I0054409

# NEW RULES FOR THE

# 6-FIGURE JOB SEARCH

## How to Position Yourself for Success

# TRISH McGRATH

**PYP**

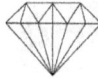

Copyright © 2022 Trish McGrath. All rights reserved.

No part of this publication shall be reproduced, transmitted, or sold in whole, or in part, in any form without prior written consent of the author, except as provided by the United States of America copyright law. Any unauthorized usage of the text without express written permission of the publisher is a violation of the author's copyright and is illegal and punishable by law. All trademarks and registered trademarks appearing in this guide are the property of their respective owners.

For permission requests, write to the below address:

PYP Academy Press
141 Weston Street, #155
Hartford, CT 06141

The opinions expressed by the author are not necessarily those held by PYP Academy Press.

Ordering Information: Quantity sales and special discounts are available on quantity purchases by corporations, associations and nonprofit organizations. For details, please contact the author at trish.mcgrath@edgecareersolutions.com.

Edited by: Andrea Glass
Cover design by: Nelly Murariu
Typeset by: Nelly Murariu

Printed in the United States of America.
ISBN: 978-1-955985-37-6 (Hardcover)
ISBN: 978-1-955985-36-9 (Paperback)
ISBN: 978-1-955985-38-3 (Ebook)

Library of Congress Control Number: 2021924742

First edition, January 2022

The information provided within this book is for general informational and educational purposes only. If expert assistance is required, the services of appropriate professionals should be sought. The author makes no representations or warranties, express or implied, about the completeness, accuracy, reliability or availability with respect to the information, products, services or related graphics contained in this book for any purpose. The advice and strategies found within may not be suitable for every situation. This work is sold with the understanding that neither the author nor the publisher can be held responsible for results yielded from the advice in this book.

# CONTENTS

# Dedication

*This book is dedicated to my husband Jon, whose love and support gave me the confidence to escape an unhealthy work environment and build the life I love, and to Gary Shea, whose sudden death was the wake-up call I needed to take action. Gary, your spirit lives on in the people whose lives I touch.*

# CHAPTER 1

# Plan, Prepare, Take Action!

T aking a proactive approach to your career is the first step towards long-term success and happiness. I don't want you to have to learn through trial and error or, worse, sabotage yourself by relying on outdated advice. Your time is far too valuable for that. Why leave your success to chance when you can, instead, use proven strategies that have been successful for so many others? Everything you need is right here in a process-focused quick read to help you navigate today's complex job search.

I'm on a mission to help as many people as I can live happier professional lives. My mid-career motivation to become a career coach were the tremendous number of people stuck in jobs that made them unhappy and too many talented people out of work simply because they didn't understand the new world of digital job search. I wrote this book for you — to reduce your frustration with simple, straightforward advice based on current industry best practices, which will help you land a job you enjoy that pays you what you're worth.

In *New Rules for the 6-Figure Job Search*, I reveal the insider secrets you need to succeed and share the step-by-step process that has helped hundreds of my career coaching clients define, achieve and enjoy career success. Proven tips and techniques, not shortcuts or tricks to rig the system. That's not who I am, and more importantly, you would be doing yourself a disservice if you conducted your job search in that manner.

While there's no one foolproof plan, there *are* specific actions that will increase your odds of success. You will see that each step of the process builds consecutively upon the other. (Which means you can't skip any, sorry! But that's okay.) To prepare you for success and help you achieve your goal, I've broken down the process into manageable, bitesize pieces to keep you moving forward.

Regardless of your role, industry or end goal (promotion, career change or a new job after a layoff), the process is essentially the same:

❶ **PLAN**
Clarify your short-term and long-term career goals

❷ **PREPARE**
Articulate your value and lay out a roadmap

❸ **TAKE ACTION**
Work the plan, completing every step in order

Like a three-legged stool, each part of the job search process is equally important, and they work together. If your planning, preparation or effort are weak, your job search will not be as successful.

Because I truly want you to succeed, I won't waste your time by telling you what to do in theory and then leaving you to fend for yourself. In my typical direct, no-nonsense fashion, I'll teach you *how* to do it with specific actions in logical order. Check off each as you complete it, and you'll be able to see your progress towards your goal!

---

### JOB SEARCH CHECKLIST

- ☐ Target Role Identified
- ☐ Compelling Conversation Opener
- ☐ Resume
- ☐ LinkedIn Profile
- ☐ Cover Letter
- ☐ Interview Prep
- ☐ Strategic Job Search Plan
- ☐ Conducting Your Job Search
- ☐ Tracking Your Progress

---

The career management philosophy I share with my clients is how I live my life and it has served me well: *Your results depend upon the quantity and quality of your effort. You must continually assess your progress and occasionally recalibrate to keep moving in the right direction.* So, if your job search isn't winning you job offers, please stop what you're doing. Pause and look to see where the process might be broken. Is it your resume, the types of jobs you're targeting, a lack of networking or your interview performance? It may be that only one step needs fine-tuning or possibly you need an entirely new approach. Fix what's not working and you'll improve your results. I promise. And you're not alone. I'm here to help you and I love this stuff!

Life can be an interesting journey. It's rarely a direct route; more often than not, it's a circuitous path with a few bumps and detours along the way. But that's what makes us who we are — an accumulation of our experiences, right? Because the career coaching relationship is personal and built on trust, I'd like to share a little of my story with you.

I was raised in a loving, reasonably normal family by parents who told me that I could be anything I wanted to be. All it took was hard work, perseverance and doing what's right. Hey, a little luck doesn't hurt either. I don't think I was ever told to pick a career that I loved. I did pretty well in college and over the years, I worked in some interesting corporate jobs, most of which I enjoyed. I learned a lot from some great and some not-so-great bosses and made a decent living. But it took me decades to find what brought me to life because I didn't even know that I should be looking!

When I was in my mid-40s and attending the funeral for a friend's father, I asked myself what legacy I wanted to leave. This man was one of those old-fashioned, small-town doctors who made house calls and accepted baked goods when his clients couldn't pay. He was a pillar of his community, and the outpouring of love and gratitude at his funeral was inspiring. I had always worked hard and was proud of my contributions, but I knew I wasn't making the world a better place. I realized that I wanted more — in my life and in my job. I wanted to be helping people in a meaningful way. My one gift was writing resumes. Most people don't find this interesting, but to me, it is like creating a commercial. Since a young adult, I had helped dozens of friends and family members get great jobs and wondered if I could use this ability to help others in a more formal manner.

Soon after, I attended a volunteer recruitment fair and met the director of a local domestic violence program. Not sure how I could help, I asked her if she thought her clients could use my resume writing or job search assistance. She eagerly responded that several current shelter residents needed jobs to help them regain their financial independence. A survivor myself, I had been lucky to have family help me escape an abusive relationship while in college. Not everyone is so fortunate. The thought of helping another survivor rebuild their life free of violence was life-affirming! I knew what I wanted to do, what I had to do. This was my calling.

So, I trained to become a Certified Domestic Violence Victim Advocate and started meeting with the women in groups and one-on-one sessions. There was some resistance at first, as many of the women were dejected and not sure they had anything of value to offer. But, as time went on, I was able to build their trust and pull out of them their strengths, skills, interests and employment experience. I then created professional-looking resumes that built up their self-confidence and helped them land new jobs. Being able to help these women feel good about themselves and get back on their feet just blew me away! I had never felt this sense of emotional reward working in any of my corporate jobs. Lightbulb moment!

I didn't want just a job. I wanted to do work that mattered!

Realizing I could use my writing skills to help others and bring in some extra money, I invested in my future by joining a professional association for resume writers that offered industry-recognized training. In April 2009, I built a website and launched my business: The Resume Resource (which was rebranded six years later as Edge Career Solutions to reflect my growing expertise and the range of career services I offered). I worked with clients at night and on weekends, building my business and mastering my craft while I kept my day job.

Work was becoming increasingly stressful as there were continual layoffs due to the recession. The harder I worked, the more extra duties my mercurial boss piled on. Somehow, I got it all done but I got lost along the way. The long hours and breakneck pace were taking a toll on me physically and mentally. I was miserable at work and, believe me, not much fun to be around at home either. My kids, partner, parents and everyone who knew me were genuinely concerned for my sanity. As was I. It was a pretty unsettling time. Was this the way it was supposed to be? Was this all life offered?

As time wore on, I was more stressed and could feel my spirit weakening a little more every day. In late February 2011, I was near my breaking point when the unthinkable happened. A good friend who was under a lot of stress at his own job took his life. Wham! It was just the wake-up call I needed. Suddenly, I could clearly see my own downward spiral and realized that not only did I deserve better, but I had to get out while I still could! I finally understood that I needed a job where I was valued and treated well. I had the right to be happy and was determined to make it happen.

A few days later, I submitted written notice to leave the company at the end of May. To make this a successful career move, I gave myself three months to plan and prepare. Energized and optimistic, I was no longer held back by uncertainty or fear of financial instability. I knew I was smart and hardworking and could be successful working for myself. More importantly, I finally realized that my happiness, mental and physical health were more valuable than a steady paycheck. My destiny was now in my own hands as opposed to external forces over which I had no control. The prospect was unnerving but exhilarating! On my last day, I said goodbye and ran towards my future.

Fast forward ten years. I'm a respected career transition coach with a nationwide practice serving job seekers across dozens of industries. I've developed a highly effective coaching process that has helped hundreds of people clarify what they want to do in the next chapter of their career and actually achieve it. My clients earn promotions and get great new jobs because together we make it happen. We plan, prepare and only then do we take action (a core theme you'll see echoing throughout this book).

While starting fresh has its ups and downs, I have never once regretted leaving the job that made me so miserable. I am living proof that you can reinvent yourself in a rewarding second-act career. I'm now thriving in a purpose-driven life and have never been happier. I know what it's like to be stuck in a job you don't enjoy and feel like you don't have any options. This inspires me every day to help others find the same level of career satisfaction that I now have.

I wrote *New Rules for the 6-Figure Job Search* because I know there are a lot of DIYers out there who just need a few pointers and to be steered in the right direction. I want to help as many people as I can, so I'm sharing the insider secrets, latest industry best practices and techniques that I use with my own clients. Designed to be a blueprint for success, I break down each component of the job search process into manageable, sequential steps with tips to help you get it right the first time.

Jumping ahead to the end of the book in hopes of quickly landing a new job may be tempting, but you know that's not the way it works. A successful job search takes clear, intentional action. To get you to your goal faster, I've strategically laid out each step of your job search. Like a chain that's only as strong as its weakest link, you must optimize every part of your job search to achieve the best results.

As I take the mystery out of your job search, you'll be able to see that it's actually quite a simple process. Take note: simple doesn't mean easy; it means not complicated. I'll show you how it's also quite doable. With a clear vision, the right preparation and a well laid out plan, you can achieve your professional goals.

In their rush to get a job, I see many people jump right into their job search before they're ready. They do what they think makes sense and then wonder why it's not working. Preparation is critical to achieving your goal because you can't take action until you know where you're going *and* how you'll get there. Today's digital job market is completely different from any previous job search you may have conducted. It requires a contemporary strategy and knowledge of modern hiring practices. That's why I frequently speak with recruiters and hiring managers, study industry trends and take specialized training throughout the year.

Imagine you want to take a trip. Before you can make your travel plans, you need to know where and when you're going, right? Otherwise, how will you know if you should book an airline ticket or gas up the car? Should you pack for a ski trip or a day at the beach? Once you've planned out your destination and completed your preparations, you can set out on your adventure.

I know there's an overwhelming amount of career advice out there and it's hard to separate facts from myths. I'm here to cut through that noise and share with you some of the strategies I use with my own clients with great results. I'm going to walk you step-by-step through my entire job search system to give you back some of your time so you can focus on the things in life that matter. Ready to turn things around? Let's jump in.

# CHAPTER 2

# Goal Setting / Determining Your Target Role

Before you can start writing your resume or take the first step in your job search, you need to decide your job target. What job title do you want? In what industry? What's your desired scope of responsibilities? I find it most effective to first determine your ultimate role and then reverse engineer your job search to achieve it. If you try to skip this step, you won't know which companies to pursue or which of your qualifications to highlight.

Don't let fear of setting a long-term goal hold you back or worry if you don't have a clear picture of what you want. Nothing in life is perfect and you can always fine-tune your goal (or completely change your mind) as you explore different options and gather new information. A general direction or "soft target" is all you need to get started.

I've found that self-awareness is key to overall career happiness. I believe there are right-fit roles for each of us — ones that align with our values, personal strengths, natural and acquired skills. Sure, you *can* do many things but when you're in a job that fits with who you are inside, it generally comes easier to you, and you'll be more successful. Even if you already know the type of job you want, realizing what's important to you can help you identify the specific roles and environments in which you thrive. Sometimes it is closer than you think.

Many people find themselves frustrated by jobs that don't align with their natural workstyles. Take my client, Joe, for example. Throughout his tech career, he enjoyed troubleshooting and resolving complex software issues. Over the years, he rose to the rank of technical support manager where he earned a decent salary with frequent bonuses. But as time went on, he was no longer inspired by his job and was looking to pivot into a new direction. He came to me for help determining the right move for the next chapter of his career.

Through our career assessments and coaching sessions, Joe realized that he still loved technology, it was just his particular role that made him feel stagnant. He spent most days in meetings, far removed from the daily tech challenges he enjoyed. Joe wanted to get back in the mix and solve the problems, not just delegate tasks and generate reports. As there was no such opportunity for him with his current employer, he sought a hands-on technology leadership role with a competitor and was hired soon after. I am happy to share that four years later, Joe is still working at that company and is excited to go to work every day.

## Identifying Your Right-Fit Role(s)

Using honest self-reflection, think about your strengths and personal characteristics — not qualities you wish you had or ones you think an employer might value. That won't be of much help to you. You want to pinpoint who you truly are inside.

Ask yourself what types of things make you happy and bring you the most satisfaction. What are your preferred communication and work styles? Would you rather communicate in writing, on the phone or in-person? Do you like to work alone or as part of a team? A variety of tools can help you through this process, from online surveys and free self-service tools to formal personality assessments like the MBTI®, StrengthsFinder® and DiSC®, which are administered and interpreted by professionals. I administer the MBTI® to many of my clients who find it helpful for articulating their natural tendencies. Be wary of books or websites that dictate which jobs you *should* pursue. You don't want to be pigeonholed or limit your options, although suggestions for the types of roles that might align with how you operate best can help guide your career exploration.

An easy way to start identifying your skills is to consider the activities that come naturally to you and the knowledge you've developed throughout your career. Think about tasks you gravitate towards and ones that are frequently assigned to you based upon your expertise. For instance, are you able to detect statistical errors? Can you persuade people to see your point of view? Equally important are your areas of weakness and tasks you *don't* like. Not strong in math? Accept that and choose a role where numbers don't play a big factor. It might be helpful to look back over previous positions you've held and think about the aspects you enjoyed the most and those you disliked. Use this same lens when you're researching potential careers and reading job descriptions.

How would you categorize your areas of expertise? Do you like writing, conducting research or crunching numbers? Are you more of a behind-the-scenes person, or do you enjoy customer-facing roles? Do you want to manage others, or do you prefer being an individual contributor responsible for your own work? There are right-fit and wrong-fit jobs for everybody and too often people are unhappy because they're in the wrong type of role. Dig deep and think about the work situations and cultures in which you've been the most comfortable and productive. Even small details can contribute to your overall happiness and satisfaction.

Hard skills are technical skills related to your job or industry that are learned through experience or training. These are the process-oriented skills you apply to perform the functions of your job. They're typically measurable competencies that you can develop and enhance through practice. Hard skills can be role-specific, like making journal entries or broader areas of knowledge like general ledger accounting. Many hard skills are transferrable between roles. If you're looking to switch careers, you'll want to emphasize your business-neutral skills that can be applied to different types of roles like customer service or Microsoft Excel.

Soft skills are intangible, non-technical skills relating to your personality traits, mindset and habits. They can impact how successful you are in your job. Employers want people who can make logical decisions, work well under pressure and are open to feedback. Other desirable characteristics include self-awareness, a growth mindset, the ability to communicate clearly and get along well with others. Emotional intelligence and adaptability are becoming increasingly important to hiring managers, as these qualities are frequently tied to an employee's ability to take on more responsibilities.

While technical skills can be taught, soft skills are part of who you are. You can work to develop skills like time management and the ability to collaborate, but in general, soft skills are your natural behaviors. I consider these to be "success skills" as they are, many times, what set you apart from your competitors. The higher ranking the role, the more important soft skills are, so be sure to highlight them in your Compelling Conversation Opener (more on this later), resume and LinkedIn profile.

Let's start with a simple activity to help you determine what you know now and what you may need help figuring out.

| SOFT SKILLS | HARD SKILLS |
|---|---|
|  |  |
|  |  |
|  |  |
|  |  |
|  |  |
|  |  |
|  |  |
|  |  |
|  |  |
|  |  |
|  |  |

| TASKS I LIKE TO DO | WHAT I NEVER WANT TO DO AGAIN |
|---|---|
|  |  |
|  |  |
|  |  |
|  |  |
|  |  |
|  |  |
|  |  |
|  |  |
|  |  |
|  |  |
|  |  |
|  |  |
|  |  |

In addition to determining what you'd like to do on the job, you should also consider your personal needs and priorities at this point in your life. Do you want to work remotely, and if so, how often? If you're early in your career, do you want an opportunity that can expose you to a variety of roles within your field or provide a mentor? Would you like to travel, or do you prefer to be home every night with your family? Is a higher salary more important to you than a flexible work schedule? Your answers to these types of questions can help clarify where you might be happiest. And yes, you do deserve to be happy in your job.

**PRO TIP:** Imagine the perfect day on your next job. Where would you be working? What would you be doing? Which of your skills would you be using? How would you feel? If this picture doesn't look anything like your job today, can you pinpoint what's missing?

## Career Exploration

Thanks to technology, exploring new careers has never been easier. Today, you don't have to actually try out a job to see if you'd like it. One of my favorite resources for career exploration is O*NET OnLine, which accesses the US Department of Labor's database of occupational information. It offers thousands of detailed job descriptions and tools that match specific skills and interests to occupations. You can learn minute details about the job that few postings would share. For instance, you may not know that as a CNC Operator you would probably be on your feet the entire day, standing next to a loud machine and watching multiple computer screens. If the system indicated there was a problem, you would respond and take corrective action. Learning specific details like that can help you determine if a job might be a good fit for you. O*NET also includes a role-specific economic outlook based on current labor data, as well as the training or education that may be required.

Online job search engines like www.linkup.com can be quite informative too. The database gathers job market data directly from employer websites every day, so the verified job listings are current. Some of the larger aggregate job sites contain a mixture of valid, fake and outdated postings. It would be a shame if you wasted your time and effort applying for jobs that didn't exist or closed months ago. Although externally advertised job postings represent only a fraction of all open positions, reading online job descriptions can help you learn about a variety of different careers. You can do a keyword search by skill, job title or company name. I recommend that new Linkup users search first by only their zip code to see the wide range of jobs available in their local area.

Career conversations are another way to find out what it's really like to work in a specific job. These interactions were previously called informational interviews, but that term has developed a negative connotation because most people don't like interviews. You'll usually have better luck if you ask someone to spend a few minutes of their time answering questions about their career in a short conversation. It's important that you speak with someone who's currently working in your job of interest, not a hiring manager or recruiter who may not be as familiar with the role. Job descriptions are written to attract candidates, so they rarely mention negative aspects of the position. However, a person who's in the same, or a similar, role today can share the realities of the job. You may want to ask them how they got their start, what their typical day entails or if they like it. You may also be curious about growth opportunities or training you could take now to improve your candidacy.

## Determining Where You're Most Marketable

Once you've figured out the type of job you like, you need to find out where the opportunities lie. It comes down to who needs what you offer and who will pay you to do it. Which industries, and what types of companies? Do your skills apply to more than one role? Is more training or education needed or could you perform the duties of the role today? Knowledge is power. Rather than guessing or assuming you know the answer, gather the data so you don't waste your time or effort. Fortunately, this information is readily available online and through career conversations with professionals in the field.

## When and Where?

The next step is to determine your hiring timeline. When would you like to be in your new role? Are there any external factors you need to consider, like the payout of your annual bonus at your current employer or waiting until the end of the fiscal year? I encourage you to have realistic expectations. These days, a typical job search can take anywhere from 2-9 months, although your actual results can vary depending upon your industry, level of seniority and effort you put in. You should also consider where you want to be 1, 5 and 10 years from now. It might make sense to identify steppingstone positions to help you advance to your ultimate goal.

How about your geographic area? Are your best opportunities in major metropolitan areas or spread out across the country? Online market research, trade publications and the US Department of Labor provide valuable information that can help you gain an accurate picture of the current employment market. Relying on online job boards can be misleading; you don't want to waste your time chasing a dead end. Do you want to relocate? For most industries, you shouldn't have to. But if you *do* want to relocate, there may be other factors to take into account, like having to sell your house or waiting until the end of the school year for your family's sake. Gathering intel and answering these questions before you launch your job search can reduce frustrating false starts.

## What Do You Want to Do and Where Do You Want to Work?

Here's a sample of a soft target goal to get your job search started:

**Function:** Software Development
**Title:** Director of Software Engineering
**Industry:** FinTech
**Type of Company:** Any size
**Location:** Dallas/Fort Worth area

A more specific goal will help you identify the right opportunities faster.

**Function:** Software Development
**Title:** Director of Software Engineering
**Industry:** FinTech
**Type of Company:** Payroll processing, US company w global footprint, >1,000 employees

**Location:** Dallas/Fort Worth area; within a 30-minute commute of zip code 75063

**Scope of Role:** Driving high profile development projects and leading team of programmers using IBM Watson to integrate AI into business processes

**Compensation:** $190-$210K salary, 25% bonus opportunity, medical benefits, 4 weeks PTO, 401(k) or similar retirement plan

# CHAPTER 3

# Articulating Your Value

Once you have your job target identified, the first step towards making it happen is to develop your messaging. When asked, are you able to clearly articulate how you help organizations succeed? Most people can't. But you do need to have a concise introduction ready because you never know when an opportunity may present itself.

It all starts with your personal brand. Many people come to me confused about personal or professional branding. Simply put, it's your reputation and what you're known for — or would like to be known for. It's also called your unique selling proposition (USP) or unique value proposition (UVP). It's the value you offer an organization and how you stand out from your peers.

How would you describe what you bring to the table that other people don't? Have you developed specific expertise or specialized in a certain area? Do you have a unique background or perspective that differentiates you from your competitors? Your personal brand is the foundation for how you'll market yourself to potential employers. It's your superpower.

## Compelling Conversation Opener

Ditch the boring elevator pitch! A Compelling Conversation Opener (CCO) is the new, more effective networking introduction that invites two-way interaction. In the traditional elevator speech, one person would spout out as much information about themself as they could in 60-90 seconds. As you have no doubt experienced, people tend to tune out these one-sided sales pitches. Here's a better way to share information about yourself and initiate conversation.

Because most networking today is conducted virtually via video conferencing, being ready with a succinct introduction will help you make professional connections. Your CCO is your digital handshake and the crux of your personal brand. Because people hire people they know, like and trust, the best way to get to know someone is to speak *with* them, not *at* them. What would you like people to know about your career accomplishments? What might make you memorable? Present yourself positively in terms of how you help organizations succeed now and in the future — not what you used to do.

Here's an exercise to help you create your Compelling Conversation Opener.

## The CCO Formula

Who I am: _____

Who I help: _____

The results I deliver: _____

How I do it: _____

### Step #1: Who I am

⮑ Desired next job title, designation or area of expertise

⮑ Write this in the present tense to help position yourself for your next role. Don't focus on what you did in the past.

*Example: I'm a senior materials engineer.*

### Step #2: Who I help

⮑ If you help people, who are they — consumers, first-time home buyers, students, retirees, parents?

⮑ If you help organizations, describe them by industry, size, their core business, etc.

*Example: I help ceramic bearing ball manufacturers who serve the global aerospace industry.*

### Step #3: The results I deliver

➲ Something specific your employer/client needs or wants

➲ Do you help people achieve financial freedom, make healthy lifestyle choices, or help organizations gain market share, lower operational costs, launch new products?

*Example: I enable the organization to gain market share by delivering higher quality products than their competitors.*

### Step #4: How I do it

➲ What differentiates you from the competition?

➲ What do you do better than your peers?

*Example: I specialize in developing precision ceramic materials that can withstand higher temperatures and maintain structural integrity longer.*

### Step #5: Weave it into a cohesive introduction

➲ Add more details and make it interesting

➲ Goal: no more than 30 seconds long, <100 words

➲ Try to focus on the value you deliver an organization

➲ Leave them wanting more information so they'll want to continue the conversation

Sample Introductions for Different Situations:

### Sample in-person or online networking introduction

"Hi, I'm Jordan Jobseeker, a senior materials engineer who helps ceramic ball manufacturers gain market share by delivering higher quality products than their competitors. I specialize in developing precision ceramic materials for aerospace applications that can withstand higher temperatures and maintain their structural integrity longer. I contribute to organizational profitability by focusing on continually improving product quality and durability. If you have any questions about me or the high-tech ceramic products I help develop, just let me know. Thank you."

### Sample post-introduction response to "So, tell me about yourself" or "What do you do?":

"Specializing in materials engineering, I help ceramic ball manufacturers gain market share by delivering higher quality products than their competitors. I develop precision ceramic materials for aerospace applications that can withstand higher temperatures and maintain their structural integrity longer. I contribute to organizational profitability by focusing on continually improving product quality and durability."

After you compose your CCO, I recommend you repeatedly practice saying it aloud until it easily rolls off your tongue in a conversational manner, so you'll be prepared to introduce yourself when an opportunity arises. You may find it helpful to record your CCO using your phone's voice memo feature. Don't be surprised if you need to revise and rerecord it a few times until you like the way it sounds. The next step is to compose a few follow-up speaking points to answer any questions or continue the conversation.

Now that you have determined how you'd like to be portrayed and can concisely convey what you offer an organization, rebranding your resume will be easier. Consider your resume and LinkedIn profile extensions of your CCO. All 3 pieces work together to solidify your professional brand, so make sure you convey a consistent message with everything you do.

# CHAPTER 4

# Writing a Resume that Wins Interviews

Your resume is perhaps the most influential document you'll ever write. In an instant, it can make or break how people view you. It can either present you as a respected professional or cause you to look like a wannabe. Elevating your resume into a top-quality career marketing document is crucial to the success of your job search as well as your overall career advancement.

If your resume isn't winning you frequent interviews, then it's simply not doing its job. The hiring process is much more complicated today. Hiring is ultra-competitive, and with so many talented people vying for the same position, you need to stand head and shoulders above other candidates. A well-written resume resonates with the reader and piques their interest — making them eager to meet you. The proper language, tone and cadence will convey your level of professionalism, and using the right keywords will show that you're highly qualified for the position. Including examples of relevant professional successes will increase your chance of winning an interview.

Resumes have changed a lot over the last few years. You can't just update your boring old work history and expect it to sell you today.

If you haven't modernized your resume, odds are it will need a major overhaul. Generic resumes don't win interviews, as many frustrated job seekers have found. You need to write your resume for the employer and address their priorities to convince them that you're a strong match for the role. But don't worry, I'll tell you how to craft your resume in a way that it targets the specific job you want.

Your resume is your commercial and its function is to position you for your next role, so it must be aspirational in nature, not historical. Don't tell your whole life story. Instead, emphasize the appropriate aspects of your professional life. One of the primary ways resumes have evolved over the last decade is the addition of a Branding Summary at the beginning that sets the stage for the reader. Right off the bat, you need to tell the reader where you would fit within their organization and the results you offer them.

Take my client David, for example. David came to me for resume help after he was passed over for promotion for the second time. The Director of Product Development at a consumer goods distributor, he had been with his company for 8 years and thought that his performance would speak for itself. After leading several successful product rollouts that exceeded revenue expectations, David believed he was a sure winner for the Regional Vice President position. He had the skills and qualifications to excel in the role, but the decision-makers did not recognize his strengths and all that he had accomplished.

Together, we put together a stellar resume that established David's professional brand, highlighted his achievements and demonstrated how he contributes to organizational performance. Through our coaching exercises, I uncovered examples of the success he delivered and used these to construct a compelling career narrative written in his voice. He shared with me that seeing his professional accomplishments documented in this way was life-affirming. He had not realized how much he had achieved throughout his career. He was very proud of his new resume, and it bolstered his confidence. He scheduled a meeting with the hiring manager, presented his resume and was granted an interview. Unfortunately, no, David did not get that job. He made it through three rounds of interviews but ultimately lost the job to a more qualified candidate. But he is now prepared for success and is pursuing other internal and external opportunities.

**PRO TIP:** You can't leave it to the reader to guess where you might fit within their organization. They'll just move on to the next resume in the pile. You need to connect the dots for them.

There are two main types of resumes: reverse-chronological and functional. The traditional reverse-chronological format is the one preferred by recruiters and hiring managers because it's easier to read. As its name implies, you list your current, or most recent, professional experience first and sequentially work backwards. Bullets under each position highlight your scope of responsibility and what you accomplished within the role. A functional resume, on the other hand, lists your skills and work experience separately. That makes it harder to determine your career trajectory, longevity with a company or what you accomplished in each position. A functional resume is a red flag for recruiters and hiring managers, possibly indicating excessive job jumping, gaps in employment or lack of experience. Since you're writing your resume for your audience, give it to them in the format they prefer – reverse-chronological.

I've encountered many different opinions regarding resume length, but most industry professionals agree that what matters most is the job seeker's ability to persuasively convey how they'd be an asset to the employer. So, if you can present your qualifications well on 1 page, great! But don't sell yourself short for the sake of brevity. I believe that most people need a 2-page resume to show they're a top performing candidate. I prefer 950 words of quality content across 2 pages, with a nice balance of white space for maximum readability.

Layout is important too. Recruiters spend 6 seconds, on average, reading a resume! That means you need to make your case quickly and convincingly. At first glance, does the reader see a modern resume format or an outdated generic template that shows a lack of effort? Did the applicant use excessive color and fancy fonts in an attempt to hide a lack of substance? Next, a rapid scan determines if the resume is professionally laid out and easy to read. Are the separate sections clearly defined? Are there concise bullets or big chunks of text? In just an instant, the recruiter is deciding, "Is reading this resume worth my time?"

FACT: Potential employers are judging you as a person and a worker when reviewing your resume. Your resume is a project you should have put a lot of effort into, editing and proofing extensively.

If it's sloppy or poorly written, the reader may question the quality of your everyday work product and habits.

The saying, "You never get a second chance to make a good first impression," is highly pertinent to your resume. The information on this one document is all the recruiter knows about you, so as they review it, they're trying to figure out what type of worker you might be.

A well-formatted resume = A neat person

An organized resume = A logical person

An error-free resume = A careful person

## What to Include and What to Eliminate

One of the most important things to keep in mind is that your resume is your primary career marketing document. It should include your best information, not everything you've ever done. It's like a first date and you have to be careful of oversharing. You want to present your best self, so the other person likes you. Once that's been accomplished, you can share things that may not be quite as positive with less fear of them running away. You do need to be honest, though. You want them to see you for who you are, not who you wish you were or think they want you to be. If you aren't authentic in your job search, you may land in a mismatched role in which you'd be unhappy, unsuccessful or both.

Your resume is intended to be a brief career narrative, not your autobiography. Include the information that shows that you're a valuable contributor to organizational success and remove anything that's irrelevant or obsolete. Keep in mind: people don't know what you can do until you tell them. Maintain focus on your target role and include the pertinent facts that show you are the perfect candidate for their opening. Once you've made your point, stop writing.

## Make It Easy for People to Contact You

You wouldn't believe how many resumes I've seen with outdated or incomplete contact information! So that you won't miss out on an opportunity, make sure you include the one best telephone number to reach you as well as a professional-sounding personal email address. One that includes only your first and last names is best (jordan.jobseeker@email.com). Too casual an email address (soccerfanatic1967@email.com) can make you look amateurish, and you never want to indicate your birth year to prevent age discrimination. Using an outdated email service provider like AOL or Hotmail can date you, as well; Gmail is a current and more age-neutral email domain. Using a work email address may make you look like a malcontent who's applying for their next job on company time, which, as you can guess, is generally not appealing to a potential employer.

**PRO TIP:** All your best information should appear on the top half of page 1, so it doesn't get missed. Put it in either your Branding Summary or your Areas of Expertise.

You no longer need to include your full mailing address on your resume; today, your city, state and zip code are enough. Many employers will only consider applicants who live within a certain commuting radius of their office, so they use location as one of the filtering criteria. If you omit this information, you may be left out of the pool of applicants for consideration. I also suggest you include your customized LinkedIn profile link (more on this later). If a recruiter is impressed with your resume, chances are they'll search your name online to learn more about you before reaching out. When someone 'Googles' you, your LinkedIn profile tends to be one of the first items in the search results. Additionally, including your profile link in the contact info on your resume will ensure that they find *your* information online rather than someone with the same or similar name.

## Branding Summary

Begin your resume with a strong branded introduction, not an objective statement. An objective is all about what you want, and they haven't been used for many years. Employers want to know *how* you can help them achieve their goals. What do *you* offer that the other candidates don't? Clearly describe the ways in which you will help the company succeed, your key differentiators and most relevant qualifications. Frontloading your resume with powerful accomplishments will engage the reader right away. You can use your CCO as the starting point for creating this summary section.

Thinking back to your self-reflection exercise and the list you made of your strengths and most positive traits, what can you add to your Branding Summary to set yourself apart from the competition? You may have similar experience and education to other candidates, so those won't help you gain the competitive edge. Avoid overused clichés like "hard-working, creative team player," "detail-oriented" and "outside the box thinking." These are still good concepts, but when phrases are overused, they become empty and make you look outdated. Even more so since the COVID-19 pandemic, employers today are looking for confident communicators who are transparent, adaptable, resilient and able to find new ways to solve problems. If you have any of these traits, play them up throughout your resume. Be honest with yourself and potential employers. Don't claim to have strengths or experience you don't have. Being deceitful on your resume will come back to bite you every time.

It can be difficult to write about yourself in a way that resonates with the reader. Many job seekers don't know what employers want to know or which information is "resume-worthy." I came across this quote recently and realized that it clearly explains why writing your own resume can be so difficult:

*You Can't Read the Label When You're Inside the Jar.*

Because you're writing your career narrative for your audience, it can be helpful to get input from others rather than writing in a vacuum. Ask other people their thoughts on your best qualities. Review past performance reviews to see how your manager described your strengths and how you contributed to the organization. Think about compliments you have received from colleagues, clients or friends. If some of this information isn't right for your resume, it might be perfect for your cover letter or the situational C-A-R stories you share during an interview.

## Sample Branding Summary

Executive-level IT professional designs cost-saving enterprise solutions for global FinTech operations. Career highlights include a seamless $636M post-merger integration of 3 SAAS platforms that delivered a 32% gain in market share and minimal attrition.

## Areas of Expertise

The next section of your resume is a bulleted list of your key competencies, used to focus the reader's attention on the most critical information. Keep in mind, these should be areas of expertise that are relevant to the role you're pursuing, not adjectives or personal attributes. For example, an accountant might include Accounts Payable, but not that they're diligent or meticulous, in this section. If you're early in your career and haven't yet developed specialized experience, a list of your transferrable skills may be more appropriate for your resume.

### Sample Areas of Expertise

| | | |
|---|---|---|
| Financial Reporting | Accounts Payable | Accounts Receivable |
| Bank Reconciliation | Internal Audits | Portfolio Management |
| General Ledger | Journal Entries | Month End Close |

## Professional Experience

Even section headings matter. Doesn't "Professional Experience" sound much more impressive than "Work History"? Every word counts on your resume, so use strong language and positive adjectives everywhere you can. Going back only 12 to 15 years, list each of your jobs in reverse-chronological order. Include the company name, city and state, position title, beginning and end years (or present for current roles) and then 3-7 bullets per job, depending on your length of employment. Your most recent jobs are typically the most important, so I suggest dedicating more resume real estate to those. After all, employers want to know what you can do for them today, not what you excelled at 10 years ago.

## Sample job entry

| Company Name, City, ST | Year to Year |
| --- | --- |

Job Title

Accomplishment bullet #1

Accomplishment bullet #2

Accomplishment bullet #3

Accomplishment bullet #4

## Company Name and Location

This part seems straightforward but can be confusing to many job seekers. Between spinoffs, mergers and acquisitions, company names can change often. I generally suggest using the company's current name followed by the previous name in parentheses — for example, Allbright Lighting Company (formerly United Luminary), City, ST. For employers with more than one location, list the city in which you primarily worked. If you were a remote employee, include the company's primary location and then indicate that you worked remotely in parentheses after your job title.

## Dates

To achieve a less cluttered resume, I prefer to omit months and only use years for beginning and end dates. However, some online applications require that you include a month, so you should keep this information handy in a master resume file in case you need it someday. Note, the dates are flush right so the reader can easily see your longevity in each position. For a clean look, be sure to use a right tab to justify your dates to the right margin rather than using multiple left tabs and spaces. Without consistent formatting, your resume can look careless and unprofessional, which in turn, might make you look like a less than desirable candidate.

**PRO TIP:** Note the word "to" rather than a dash between the years in the previous example. I recommend this practice because not everyone is meticulous about consistently adding a space before and after a dash. Formatting inconsistencies like that look sloppy. Additionally, different versions of Microsoft Word can substitute en dashes for em dashes ( -, - ).

## Accomplishment Bullets

Showing people what you can do is much more convincing than simply telling them. Hiring managers want new employees who can step in and contribute on Day One. Using quantified and qualified achievements is a terrific way to demonstrate the immediate value you offer an organization. Accomplishment statements convince the reader that you really do have the expertise they need. Employers don't want *good* employees; they want *great* ones, so confidently describe the value you deliver. Don't worry, you're not bragging when you talk about what you've achieved. You're simply sharing information about your professional wins with someone who wants to hear about them.

Rather than focusing on your tasks or duties, explain *how* the company benefitted from you doing your job so well. Removing the phrases "responsible for" and "duties included" from your resume will prompt you to focus on the impact of the work you performed. Describe significant projects you led, instances where you saved money or issues you resolved. To make it easier for the reader to appreciate your achievements, create a two-line bullet for each one starting with a strong action verb.

You can use a variety of ways to illustrate the value you add to an organization. Show employers that you truly have the experience they require by providing details on specific results you've delivered. Including background information in the example will put your accomplishment into context for the reader, while quantifying or qualifying your achievements will add impact.

Dollars, numbers and percentages are the most common ways to express quantified achievements and are most appropriate for items that can be calculated numerically, like savings, profitability, customers and sales. You can also use figures to represent ranking, time to completion, new hires, social media followers or favorable client reviews.

Reductions in cost, labor hours, time to market, production downtime, turnover or outstanding accounts would impress decision-makers, as would gains in quality, efficiency, profitability, market share and client retention. Don't forget less obvious contributions to organizational performance like improved timeliness, accuracy, collaboration or communication. Be sure to clearly explain how your efforts benefitted the company.

If you get stuck describing your accomplishments, the Challenge-Action-Result (C-A-R) method can help you explain what you helped the company achieve.

**C:** Challenge: What was the problem you addressed / goal you were pursuing?

**A:** Action: What did you do?

**R:** Result: What outcome (savings / reduction / increase / improvement) did you achieve?

*Example:*

| CHALLENGE | Overtime labor expenses continued to increase every year |
| --- | --- |
| ACTION | I developed a staggered work schedule that increased employee productivity |
| RESULT | We reduced labor costs by 12% |
| RESUME BULLET | Recognizing that overtime labor was increasing every year, proactively developed a staggered employee work schedule that reduced labor costs by 12% while maintaining high service and satisfaction levels. |

## Education

Unless you recently graduated college, your education section should be the last one on your resume. Once you have a few years of professional experience, your education becomes less significant. Listing your most recent degree first, include the degree, major, minor or concentration (if you had one), institution name, city and state. Drop education dates completely if you graduated more than 10 years ago. If you attended more than one institution, include only the one from which you graduated, unless there's something significant about your first college experience. If you attended college but didn't graduate, you can still include this on your resume but don't claim to have a degree if you don't.

### Sample education section

**(If you earned a degree)**

MS, Forensic Science, University of Massachusetts, Amherst, MA

Thesis: *ISP Techniques for Forensic Procedures and Admissibility of DNA Evidence*

**(If you did not graduate)**

Williams College, Williamstown, MA, completed 3 semesters of coursework towards a bachelor's degree in computer science

**PRO TIP:** be sure to spell out the word degree if you didn't complete yours, so your resume will make it through the ATS. [See below]

## Ongoing Training / Professional Development

List both formal and informal training to show that you continue to add to your skillset.

## Technical Skills

List the various software you use, including the version where applicable and software type, when it is uncommon. If you're in IT or a related field, you should have a separate Technical Skills section. For the rest of us, mentioning how you used specific software within your accomplishment bullets should suffice. Although strong technical skills may be a given today, employers do want to make sure new hires have the skills they need.

## Other sections to include, if appropriate

Career Highlights, Certification and Licensure, Professional Affiliations, Honors and Awards, Publications and Volunteer Activities.

## References

Please do not include references or mention they're available. That's a given. Don't waste the valuable space on your resume or date yourself with this antiquated practice.

## Applicant Tracking System Compatibility: Keywords and Formatting

Most employers use Applicant Tracking Systems (ATS) to automate and manage the hiring process. They use keyword filters to identify the most qualified applicants among the many incoming resumes. Those flagged for review are given the most attention, while the others may not even be read by a human being. You can avoid the resume black hole by formatting your resume for ATS compatibility. Don't try to fool the ATS; just follow these tips to work within them. My resume writing strategy: write for the machine first using proper keywords and formatting and the human reader second by making it visually appealing and easy to read.

## Keywords

Show that you're a highly qualified candidate by including the relevant keywords (skills, qualifications and personal attributes) for the role throughout your resume. Some ATS don't recognize synonyms or abbreviations, so try to match the language used in the job posting precisely. Where can you find the keywords? In addition to the position description, use the company website and your own knowledge and experience. If you're truly qualified for the job, you know the skills and experience required. Beware: don't just stuff keywords in where they don't belong. Use them strategically throughout your resume, in proper context, to show you're a good match for the position.

## Clean Formatting

Avoid fancy formatting to help ensure your resume will load into the ATS properly. You can use advanced formatting features on the hard copy resume you bring to an interview, but use a version with simpler formatting for online applications and any resumes sent via email.

Formatting specifics:

- The most widely accepted resume format is the Word 2003 .doc. Only upload a PDF or Word .docx if the online application system lists those as compatible formats.

- Many ATS can now handle tables, but most read the information from left to right by rows. This can combine multiple phrases together, making them hard to understand. Avoid using multiple columns for the same reason.

- Use common fonts (I like Arial) and avoid advanced formatting options like small caps or kerning.

- Solid round black bullets are fine but don't use fancy ones or sub-bullets as they look cluttered.

- Standard section headings make it easier for ATS to properly identify and parse the information. Don't combine sections for the same reason.

- No headers and footers. Most ATS can't pick up information in the document header or footer, so put your name and contact information in the body of your document.

- No graphics, pictures, symbols or special characters. While they may not jam up the ATS upload like they used to, images don't get read as data.

◗ No page borders, shapes or text boxes. You can use shading and outline to highlight important information.

◗ Please don't rush the writing, reviewing and editing of your resume; your career is far too important. And once you have a strong resume, keep it a living document by continuing to add your professional accomplishments so you'll be ready when an opportunity presents itself.

**PRO TIP:** You will look only as professional as your resume does.

Here are some powerful "action verbs" to strengthen your resume's accomplishment bullets.

## 500+ of the Best Resume Verbs

| | | |
|---|---|---|
| Accelerated | Adjusted | Arbitrated |
| Accomplished | Administered | Architected |
| Accounted | Advanced | Arranged |
| Accrued | Advised | Assembled |
| Accumulated | Advocated | Assessed |
| Achieved | Aided | Assigned |
| Acknowledged | Aligned | Assimilated |
| Acquired | Allocated | Assisted |
| Adapted | Amplified | Attained |
| Added | Analyzed | Audited |
| Addressed | Appointed | Augmented |

| | | |
|---|---|---|
| Authored | Changed | Contracted |
| Automated | Charted | Contributed |
| Avoided | Clarified | Controlled |
| Awarded | Classified | Conversed |
| Balanced | Closed | Converted |
| Bargained | Coached | Conveyed |
| Blended | Coalesced | Convinced |
| Blocked | Co-Authored | Cooperated |
| Bolstered | Coded | Coordinated |
| Boosted | Collaborated | Corrected |
| Bought | Collected | Corresponded |
| Brainstormed | Commanded | Counseled |
| Briefed | Communicated | Created |
| Brought | Compared | Critiqued |
| Brought Forth | Compelled | Culled |
| Brought Into | Compiled | Cultivated |
| Compliance | Completed | Curated |
| Brought to Light | Complied | Curtailed |
| Brought Together | Composed | Customized |
| Budgeted | Computed | Cut |
| Built | Conceived | Dealt |
| Calculated | Concentrated | Debated |
| Campaigned | Conceptualized | Debriefed |
| Capitalized | Conducted | Debugged |
| Carried Out | Confronted | Debuted |
| Case Managed | Conserved | Decided |
| Cataloged | Consolidated | Deciphered |
| Centralized | Constructed | Decreased |
| Chaired | Consulted | Deducted |
| Championed | Contacted | Defended |

| | | |
|---|---|---|
| Defined | Diversified | Enlightened |
| Delegated | Diverted | Enlisted |
| Delivered | Documented | Enlivened |
| Demonstrated | Doubled | Ensured |
| Deployed | Drafted | Entertained |
| Derived | Dramatized | Enticed |
| Designated | Drew Up | Envisioned |
| Designed | Dropped | Equalized |
| Detailed | Drove | Equipped |
| Detected | Drove Down | Established |
| Determined | Earned | Estimated |
| Developed | Economized | Evaluated |
| Devised | Edited | Examined |
| Diagnosed | Educated | Exceeded |
| Diagramed | Eliminated | Exchanged |
| Dictated | Embraced | Executed |
| Differentiated | Employed | Exhibited |
| Diminished | Empowered | Expanded |
| Directed | Enabled | Expedited |
| Discerned | Enacted | Explained |
| Disciplined | Encouraged | Explored |
| Discovered | Endeavored | Expressed |
| Discussed | Ended | Extracted |
| Dispatched | Endorsed | Fabricated |
| Dispensed | Endured | Facilitated |
| Displayed | Energized | Familiarized |
| Disproved | Enforced | Fashioned |
| Dissected | Engineered | Fielded |
| Disseminated | Enhanced | Filed |
| Distributed | Enlarged | Financed |

| | | |
|---|---|---|
| Fixed | Humored | Interacted |
| Focused | Hunted | Interpreted |
| Followed | Hypothesized | Intervened |
| Forecasted | Identified | Interviewed |
| Forged | Ignited | Introduced |
| Formalized | Illuminated | Invented |
| Formed | Illustrated | Inventoried |
| Formulated | Imagined | Investigated |
| Fostered | Imitated | Involved |
| Founded | Implemented | Itemized |
| Funded | Improved | Joined |
| Furthered | Improvised | Journeyed |
| Gained | Incited | Judged |
| Gathered | Included | Labeled |
| Gave | Incorporated | Labored |
| Generated | Increased | Launched |
| Governed | Indexed | Learned |
| Graded | Inflated | Leased |
| Graphed | Influenced | Lectured |
| Grouped | Informed | Led |
| Guided | Initiated | Lessened |
| Halted | Innovated | Leveraged |
| Handled | Inspected | Liaised |
| Harmonized | Inspired | Lifted |
| Headed | Installed | Listed |
| Helmed | Instituted | Listened |
| Helped | Instigated | Litigated |
| Highlighted | Instructed | Lobbied |
| Hired | Integrated | Located |
| Hosted | Intensified | Logged |

| | | |
|---|---|---|
| Lowered | Navigated | Piloted |
| Magnified | Negotiated | Pioneered |
| Maintained | Networked | Pipelined |
| Managed | Nursed | Planned |
| Manipulated | Nurtured | Played |
| Mapped | Observed | Practiced |
| Marginalized | Obtained | Predicted |
| Marketed | Offered | Preempted |
| Married | Officiated | Prepared |
| Mastered | Operated | Prescreened |
| Masterminded | Optimized | Prescribed |
| Maximized | Orchestrated | Presented |
| Measured | Ordered | Preserved |
| Mediated | Organized | Presided |
| Melded | Originated | Prevented |
| Memorized | Outnumbered | Prioritized |
| Mentored | Outpaced | Probed |
| Merchandised | Outperformed | Problem Solved |
| Merged | Outran | Processed |
| Met | Overcame | Produced |
| Minimized | Overhauled | Programmed |
| Mitigated | Oversaw | Prohibited |
| Mobilized | Participated | Projected |
| Modeled | Partnered | Promoted |
| Moderated | Patented | Prompted |
| Modified | Perceived | Proofread |
| Monitored | Perfected | Propelled |
| Motivated | Performed | Proposed |
| Moved | Persevered | Prospected |
| Multiplied | Persuaded | Protected |

| | | |
|---|---|---|
| Proved | Referred | Revamped |
| Provided for | Refined | Reviewed |
| Publicized | Refocused | Revised |
| Published | Regulated | Revitalized |
| Purchased | Rehabilitated | Revolutionized |
| Quadrupled | Reinforced | Rewrote |
| Qualified | Rejected | Rid |
| Quantified | Related | Risked |
| Raised | Relayed | Rolled Out |
| Rallied | Remodeled | Satisfied |
| Ran | Remunerated | Saved |
| Ranked | Renegotiated | Scanned |
| Rated | Renewed | Scheduled |
| Reached | Rented | Scored |
| Reached Out | Reorganized | Scouted |
| Read | Repaired | Screened |
| Realigned | Replaced | Scrutinized |
| Realized | Reported | Searched |
| Reasoned | Repositioned | Secured |
| Received | Represented | Selected |
| Recognized | Reproduced | Shaped |
| Recommended | Researched | Sharpened |
| Reconciled | Reshaped | Shattered |
| Recorded | Resolved | Shaved |
| Recruited | Responded | Showcased |
| Rectified | Restored | Showed |
| Redesigned | Restructured | Shrank |
| Reduced | Resumed | Simplified |
| Reestablished | Retrieved | Simulated |
| Refereed | Reunited | Slashed |

| | | |
|---|---|---|
| Solved | Supervised | Tripled |
| Sorted | Supported | Troubleshot |
| Sought | Surpassed | Turned |
| Sourced | Surveyed | Uncovered |
| Sparked | Sustained | Understood |
| Spearheaded | Symbolized | Undertook |
| Specialized | Synchronized | Unified |
| Specified | Synthesized | United |
| Spoke | Systematized | Unraveled |
| Staffed | Tabulated | Unveiled |
| Staged | Talked | Updated |
| Standardized | Targeted | Upgraded |
| Started | Taught | Upheld |
| Steered | Terminated | Used |
| Stimulated | Tested | Utilized |
| Stood Up | Told | Vacated |
| Storyboarded | Took | Validated |
| Straightened | Topped | Verbalized |
| Strategized | Toured | Verified |
| Streamlined | Traced | Visualized |
| Strengthened | Tracked | Volunteered |
| Stressed | Trained | Waged |
| Stretched | Transcribed | Washed |
| Studied | Transferred | Weighed |
| Submitted | Transformed | Widened |
| Substantiated | Translated | Withdrew |
| Succeeded | Transmitted | Won |
| Suggested | Traveled | Worked |
| Summarized | Treated | Wrote |
| Superseded | Trimmed | Yielded |

# CHAPTER 5

# Accelerating Your Search with LinkedIn®

Before internet technology, a job search consisted of scouring newspaper classified ads and printing your resume on expensive paper. Applicants then had two options: walk into a local business, introduce yourself to the hiring manager and hand them your resume or send it to the company via US mail. Fortunately, these slow and costly approaches have been replaced by online tools that increase your reach, enable immediate communications and provide 24/7 access to global information. Employers now post (some) open positions online, where job seekers can search for and then apply for them. Another major industry change occurred when employers started proactively hunting passive candidates — those people not actively looking for a new position. Recruiters aren't just waiting for you to submit your resume anymore. They're searching online for the most qualified candidates out there. This makes the already tight job market even more competitive. Not only are job seekers competing against other applicants, but they're also being compared to their peers across the industry. Today, online platforms are the most effective way to connect job seekers with recruiters, hiring managers and other decision-makers. Outdated search tactics just don't cut it. That's why you need to be on LinkedIn.

**PRO TIP:** You've embraced technology in nearly every other aspect of your life, so why not to advance your career? New job search rules require new tools.

With 740 million global users as of 2021, LinkedIn has established itself as the leading professional networking platform as well as the preferred job search tool for recruiters and job seekers alike. It's a place for professionals to meet, build relationships, share information and search for opportunities. It has also become a reliable source of news, events and analysis. Still not convinced? Industry sources say that between 87% and 95% of recruiters use LinkedIn to find qualified employees. There are 3 million US jobs posted on the platform every month and 20 million companies have a LinkedIn presence. Job seekers are big fans too: studies report that 3 people are hired through LinkedIn every minute and 35.5 million people have been hired by a person they connected with on the site.

What does this mean for you? It means that you absolutely must have an active LinkedIn presence to gain a competitive edge over other job seekers. Even if you're not looking for a new position today, you should build and nurture your professional network now before you may need it for a job search. If you want to be found, you need to be where recruiters and hiring managers are looking for you, which is LinkedIn. I require that all my clients join LinkedIn because, in my professional opinion, regardless of your industry, role or level of experience, if you're not on LinkedIn, you're basically invisible. The digital job search is here to stay, so jump on board. As a LinkedIn profile writer and trainer, I help my clients quickly get up to speed and provide helpful tip sheets. At the request of my less tech-savvy clients, I now offer hands-on LinkedIn lessons via Zoom as well.

Adding LinkedIn's social networking capabilities to your job search will boost your results exponentially. It helps you expand your reach beyond your immediate sphere of influence and learn about openings before they're advertised outside the company. If you haven't yet ventured into this brave new digital world, don't worry. The system is user-friendly and reasonably priced. I personally use and advocate for, the free user account, although paid membership levels do offer added functionality. Even as a LinkedIn power user, I find that I can do everything I need to on the platform without paying the hefty subscription fee.

The secret to maximizing LinkedIn as a job search tool lies in three acronyms: SEO, KLT and TOM. Keeping these three concepts in mind as you use LinkedIn will help increase your visibility.

➲ **SEO:** Search engine optimization is keyword-driven, so having the right keywords throughout your profile will help you rank higher in recruiters' search results. These keywords are the skills and qualifications recruiters might use as search terms to find suitable candidates.

➲ **KLT:** People do business with people they know, like and trust. Don't just add connections to your network; start conversations and build relationships. Be approachable and highlight your expertise by sharing valuable information. Be friendly, helpful and genuine.

⊃ **TOM:** Stay top of mind with your connections through frequent LinkedIn activity. Someone may not have or know of a position for you right now, but you want them to remember you when they do. So periodically seeing your profile in their newsfeed will keep you TOM.

## Profile Best Practices

In a competitive market, managing your online reputation can be the difference between advancing your career and stagnation. Your LinkedIn profile is a powerful way to promote your personal brand. It should be a three-dimensional snapshot of you as a professional that lets people get to know the person behind the resume. Your profile should complement your resume. While they share most of the same information, the tone and overall feel of your profile should be more conversational, so the reader feels that you're speaking to them. This is your opportunity to tell your career story and let other LinkedIn users get to know you. Make your profile interesting so they want to learn more.

What should you include? Most of the profile sections are keyword searchable, so be sure to include the top skills and qualifications that a recruiter would use to search for someone in your role. Remember, you want to appear high in their search results, not lost on page eight. So, include the most highly desired qualifications throughout your profile.

Your profile must be "100% complete" for you to be considered a serious candidate and attract the attention of recruiters. The Profile Strength Meter measures your profile status based upon its relevant content. To reach "All Star" status, you need information in your About, Experience and Education sections, as well as a photo.

Many job seekers I work with are concerned for their privacy, which is surely something we all need to worry about. However, you have complete control over what information people see because you're the person building your profile. You decide what to share about yourself and you can use strategies to keep your activity under the radar if you're conducting a stealth search and don't want to alert your current employer.

## LinkedIn Profile Sections

| BASIC INFORMATION | ADDITIONAL SECTIONS |
|---|---|
| Headline / Tagline | Featured (Media, Links, Posts, Articles) |
| Headshot | Licenses And Certifications |
| Background Banner Image | Honors And Awards |
| Advice For Contacting You | Courses |
| Industry (Selected from LinkedIn's Database) | Publications / Projects / Patents |
| Location | Professional Organizations |
| About | Volunteer Experience |
| Vanity / Customized Public Profile URL | Recommendations |
| Experience | Companies You Follow |
| Education | Schools You Follow |
| Skills & Endorsements | Groups |

## Optimizing each profile section

### Your Name

You have quite a bit of flexibility regarding how you would like your name to appear on your profile. If it's professional sounding, you can use a nickname rather than your full name. For example, my legal name is Patricia, but I'm known by my preferred name, Trish. Adding your middle initial may be helpful if your name is common. You can also add a former name, suffix or professional designation (certification, license or advanced degree). A recently added feature is the ability to record your name to help people pronounce it properly, which can alternatively be used to add a short introductory message to your profile like I do.

### Headshot

I encourage you to include your picture on your profile because LinkedIn research shows profiles with photos receive 26 times more views than those without and are nine times more likely to receive connection requests. You don't need to pay for a professional headshot, but please don't upload a selfie or webcam photo if you want to be taken seriously. It's as easy as having someone use your cell phone camera to take your picture when you're dressed in attire appropriate for your industry. Avoid distracting backgrounds, make sure you're the only one in the photo and crop it to show from your shoulders up.

This should not be a glamour shot; your goal is to look smart, approachable and professional. You want to make connections and build genuine relationships on LinkedIn, so be transparent and open about who you are. It's not worth trying to hide your age;

they'll find that out eventually. A profile that is 100% complete is more likely to show up in search results than an incomplete one, so not having a LinkedIn headshot might hinder your job search. Additionally, recruiters sourcing candidates on LinkedIn report that they're less likely to contact people without photos.

## Background Banner Image

Adding a colorful and visually appealing background image can prompt other LinkedIn users to stop scrolling and click on your profile to see more. To help people picture you in your role, upload a good quality, high-resolution photo that pertains to your field. Avoid boring stock photos. Many websites offer free accounts for downloading high quality royalty-free images. My favorite is www.unsplash.com.

## Headline

A catchy tagline is valuable for branding purposes. This prominent profile field appears right under your name where it easily attracts attention. LinkedIn algorithms index headline keywords higher than those in other profile fields, which gives them more weight. Don't just use your current job title (the default that you can override). Your profile is your commercial, so make it memorable with a keyword-rich headline that includes your area of expertise and unique value proposition. Only the first part of your headline is visible until someone actually clicks on your profile, so put the most important words at the beginning, like the results you deliver or the most highly desired qualifications for your role. This is one place where creativity can pay off. As an example, here is mine (which I change often):

## Sample Profile Headline

Offering expert career advice for tough times, I prepare mid-career professionals for success. Specialties: executive career coaching for advancement, pivots and reaching the C-Suite

## About Section/Summary

According to LinkedIn, many recruiters consider your About section the most important part of your profile. Unfortunately, I see too many people aren't even using this powerful summary section because they're unsure of how to promote themselves without sounding boastful. Simply put, people want to meet the person behind the resume. Use this section to share your achievements, your excitement for your work and what differentiates you from your competition. Like your resume, your user profile should be written for your audience and aspirational in nature, not historical. It should focus on the unique value you offer an employer today and position you as the ideal candidate for your next role.

This section is an extension of your CCO — how you would introduce yourself at a professional event. A well-written summary conveys your experience, personal strengths and passion for your career. The tone should be upbeat and conversational but not too casual. This is where you can get some of your personality across and incorporate examples of career success that you might include in a cover letter. I recommend composing your profile in Microsoft Word so you can check the character count, grammar and spelling as you edit. Keep in mind: one typo could cause a recruiter or hiring manager to dismiss you as a candidate.

Write your summary in the first-person narrative form rather than bullet points. You can use the entire 2,600 characters the field allows but these days summaries seem to be getting shorter. In two to three short paragraphs, tell your career story in a way that differentiates you from your peers. What's important to you and what drives your career success? How did you get to where you are today? You can describe your personal motivations, business philosophy or leadership style. Make it interesting and relatable. Your goal is to provide a snapshot of you as a professional that makes the reader want to get to know you better.

## Skills and Endorsements

You can include up to 50 skills to show that you have the qualifications your next role requires. (Although I hear LinkedIn is about to increase this to 100 skills.) While you can copy and paste content into most sections of your profile, you'll have to add your skills one by one. If the skill already exists in the LinkedIn database, the system will autocomplete it as you begin to type. Just click it when you see it appear in the dropdown menu. If you don't see a particular one you want to add, simply enter it using the "Add a New Skill" link. Once added to your profile, LinkedIn will group your skills into buckets. Pin your three most important skills to the top, and then reorder your other skills by dragging and dropping them within each category to prioritize those that are most relevant to your career going forward.

## Experience

Now that you've written a strong, compelling resume with the help of the previous chapter, you can use that document to build out the experience section of your profile. Going back the same 12 to 15 years, list the same jobs that appear on your resume making sure your job titles and dates match exactly. Most recruiters and hiring managers review LinkedIn profiles when considering who to bring in for an interview and you wouldn't want any discrepancies to hurt your chances of being selected. While your resume and profile do share most of the same information, the writing style in your profile is different because it's a different medium. Tell your professional story using complete sentences rather than bulleted fragments like on your resume.

## Education

Whether you graduated or left college before finishing your degree, you should add institutions of higher education you attended and your major/program of study. Only include the degree if you graduated and were awarded a diploma. It's best to refer to schools by their common names, as these are frequently used as search terms. When entering the name of your school, it should appear in the dropdown menu. Because this is a freeform field, people might enter names differently. You want to find the entry with the correct school logo, so you're selecting the school's actual LinkedIn page.

Once you're over 40 years of age, I recommend omitting graduation dates to keep your profile age neutral. If you graduated within the last five years or so, feel free to add the date and include honors and awards, notable projects, internships, groups and activities. GPA is only relevant for recent graduates. Once you've acquired a few years of professional experience, potential employers will be more impressed by career accomplishments than by grades.

Alumni networks and fraternity/sorority connections can be beneficial to your career at any age. These affiliations can be added in either the description or activities and societies fields within each education entry. Especially if it's well-known, consider adding your high school as well, so former classmates can reconnect. You never know who might have the perfect opportunity for you.

## Interests

To help you stay up on the latest happenings in your field (and let others know that you do), follow hashtags of interest and the official LinkedIn pages of industry thought leaders, sources of industry news and anywhere you've worked or would like to work. You can also join up to 50 LinkedIn groups. These interests are visible to others viewing your profile and should be representative of you as a professional.

## Recommendations

Recommendations from former and current supervisors, colleagues and clients provide social proof that hiring you is a good decision. LinkedIn makes it easy to request recommendations with a template message but to improve your odds you should customize the message to include where and when you worked together and a few of your major accomplishments. Depending on the individual, you may ask that they comment on a particular skill you possess, a specific project you led or a problem you solved. A variety of different recommendations can support the depth of your experience. Remember that networking is a two-way street; be sure to provide recommendations to others as well.

## Public Profile Link

When you first create your profile, the default public profile URL will have a series of random numbers and letters after your name. You can make it easier for people to find you, and not someone with the same name, by customizing your public profile URL to remove those extra characters. Ideally, your customized, or vanity, URL contains only your first and last names separated by a dash. The link must contain between 5 to 30 letters or numbers with no spaces, symbols or special characters. If your name is taken, the system will suggest similar alternatives. If you don't like those, continue to try different versions until you find one that's available. You may need to add your middle initial or professional designation (for example, Jordan-Q-Jobseeker or Jordan-Jobseeker-PMP).

**PRO TIP:** Be sure to add your vanity profile link to the contact information on your resume.

You can control how you appear when people search for you online by indicating what information you would like to make public. Because you're on LinkedIn to be found, I advise people to open up their profile by checking the "Make my public profile visible to everyone" box. That way, anyone can find your profile. This is especially important because LinkedIn profiles are now available to people not logged into the system. When someone searches your name online, your LinkedIn profile will typically be one of the first search results. Providing easy access to your profile, which is full of the professional information you provided, is a highly effective way to manage your online reputation.

## Growing Your Professional Network

The next step is to start building your network of connections. The main reason to be on LinkedIn is to interact with other people, so a wide network based on past and present relationships can expand your professional exposure. The larger your professional network, the further your reach. You never know who may know of a perfect opportunity for you and could put in a good word on your behalf.

But you can't just connect and disappear. You need to engage with people and build real relationships. Be transparent with your intentions and authentic in your interactions. A network full of contacts who know and respect you can garner introductions to hiring managers and warm job leads. Another bonus: your LinkedIn network is a contact list that's never out of date. As your connections update their profiles, you'll be kept current on their latest roles, projects and contact info.

Building your professional network doesn't have to be difficult. Start with people you know to help you get comfortable with the process before asking strangers to connect. Send connection invitations to people with whom you already have in-person relationships. After connecting with friends and family members, reach out to current and former colleagues, managers and clients. Fellow alumni and people you've met through face-to-face networking can be valuable referral sources. If you're looking to connect with well-known industry thought leaders, commenting on or re-sharing their content first can be a great way to prime the pump before sending a request. Another reason to include a headshot on your profile is that people want to see with whom they're connecting.

**PRO TIP:** Connecting with "superconnectors" can quickly expand your reach. For example, if you and I connect on LinkedIn, my 4,000+ first-degree connections would become your second-degree connections.

LinkedIn makes it easy to ask people to connect with a template message. Unless you know the person well, you should customize the invitation with a friendly message to improve the chance of them accepting. If you haven't seen the person in a while, remind them where you met or previously worked together. Personal LinkedIn profiles aren't designed for sending mass connection requests to all the people in your address book. (They do offer business memberships for sales and marketing purposes.) Rather than importing your entire contact list, it's better to send individual invitations to join your professional network as appropriate.

Once someone has accepted your invitation to connect, or you've accepted theirs, start a conversation with them. Apply the same etiquette rules that you would use for a face-to-face conversation. You probably wouldn't ask for a favor right after meeting someone in person, right? Then don't ask for one as soon as you connect online. If you're in transition, don't mention that you're looking for a job right away. It's more effective to give to others before asking for something. Be friendly, have a genuine conversation and let the relationship naturally evolve. If all goes well, the next step would be to take the conversation offline and schedule a telephone call or Zoom session. And just maybe that might lead to an in-person meeting.

Why is a strong LinkedIn network essential? Because approximately 80% of open positions are not advertised externally. This is the "hidden job market" you've probably heard so much about, where the majority of openings are filled without ever being posted online. That's why searching for open positions on job boards isn't as effective as in years past. You need to be where recruiters and hiring managers are looking for you. And for most employers, both big and small, LinkedIn is their primary hunting ground. In fact, a networking strategy that combines face-to-face and social interaction is consistently cited as the #1 way to land a new role today.

Leveraging professional relationships will propel your job search because the individuals making hiring decisions would rather speak to people that they know rather than wade through a pile of resumes from strangers. An active LinkedIn presence allows hiring managers to "meet" you and see what you offer an employer. When they repeatedly come across your name and see you engage with others in your industry, especially their peers, it provides social proof that you're someone worth knowing.

## Activity to Increase Your Visibility

You're on LinkedIn to be found, right? That means you need to be visible. In accordance with LinkedIn's constantly changing algorithms, frequent activity draws attention to your profile in two ways: it raises the prevalence of your posts within your connections' newsfeeds, and it improves your ranking among recruiters' search results as they source candidates. There are several things you can do on LinkedIn that constitute being active: adding new information to your profile, making new connections, posting content or commenting on others' posts.

Crafting thoughtful, well-written posts can highlight your expertise and boost your credibility as an authority in your field. Engaging in conversations and sharing insightful commentary to a wide LinkedIn network on a regular basis will increase your brand exposure and build name brand recognition. Frequent sharing of content and commenting on others' posts will help keep you top of mind, and being authentic allows people to get to know, like and trust you.

Sharing content online is easy. You can curate others' content; you don't have to compose original content yourself. It's as simple as copy and pasting a link to an online article. The article can either be on a reputable website or one that's already been posted on LinkedIn. The newsfeed on your LinkedIn homepage can be customized to your topics of interest and you can easily share right from there. To show your thought leadership, include a personal comment on your posts as well as others' posts. You can improve your post's visibility by adding three relevant, trending hashtags to the end of your comment.

To attract recruiters' attention, *how* you use your LinkedIn profile is as important as the story it tells. Following a strategic networking strategy, intentional LinkedIn activity can speed up your job search. Show potential employers that you understand their critical needs by re-sharing and commenting on company posts. In addition to establishing your personal brand, this is also a great way to start conversations and connect with decision-makers. Remember, your LinkedIn profile is your digital business card and represents your professional online image. Do it right and your next job just might find you.

LinkedIn is also a great tool for information gathering, like researching companies to create your target list of potential employers. Searching companies by industry and location, you can find many with LinkedIn Company Pages that provide an overview of the organization, a list of employees who have LinkedIn profiles and a link to the company website.

Speaking with people who work at a company of interest can help you determine if it might be a good fit for you personally and professionally. The platform is also a respected source of global news. It can help you stay informed on breaking news and emerging trends. You can use your LinkedIn newsfeed, online trade publications and professional organizations to keep up with your industry, which will help you stay ahead of your competition.

LinkedIn is not a "set it and forget it" networking tool. The right kind of activity on the platform can actually draw attention to your profile, which in turn can attract opportunities to you. It's a much more efficient way to manage your job search. When you apply for a job, you're using "push marketing," where you pursue individual targets, as opposed to your LinkedIn activity that "pulls" potential opportunities to you. Instead of pursuing individual jobs one at a time, network exposure is a much more efficient and effective job search strategy.

**PRO TIP:** LinkedIn is the most powerful job search tool today and many hiring experts agree that it's considered unprofessional not to have an active LinkedIn presence.

Establishing a strong online presence requires addressing these 3 aspects of LinkedIn:

1. **Your Profile** ➲ A search-optimized user profile to attract the right attention

2. **Your Network** ➲ Building relationships with a deep network of connections

3. **Your Activity** ➲ The right actions to build credibility and prominence in your field

Everybody and everything are online these days, including hiring, job search and career management. Leveraging technology will be key to finding your next opportunity, which is why your ability to master LinkedIn is so critical. I encourage you to embrace the power it offers you.

# CHAPTER 6

# Exceptional Cover Letters

F ew people enjoy writing cover letters, but they're a key part of your job search that you can't overlook. A well-written cover letter works with your resume to help you win an interview. It provides yet another opportunity to convey your expertise and set yourself apart from other candidates. Who wants to miss out on that?

Many companies use cover letters during candidate selection to identify the strongest applicants. Odds are you're one of dozens if not hundreds of applicants for one opening. The recruiter or hiring manager needs to wade through the pool of resumes to cherry-pick applicants for further review. Make it easy for them to see that you should be considered for the role.

While there's much debate as to whether recruiters actually read cover letters, they're still arguably an additional way for applicants to introduce themselves and strengthen their candidacy. So that I can offer my clients the best advice, I stay up on hiring trends and ask the recruiters I know what they look for in candidates. While nearly half told me they do not read cover letters, many stated that they do use them to weed out weak applicants. If the applicant does not follow directions by including a cover letter with their resume, they can quickly be eliminated from consideration.

If the recruiter is expecting a cover letter and you don't provide one, you might look lazy. What employer wants to hire a person they perceive as lazy? None. Since you don't know whether the person reviewing your resume likes or expects a cover letter, I recommend that you err on the side of caution and include one every time. If you're not willing to make an effort to write a cover letter for any given position, then you may want to reconsider your actual interest in that role and how it aligns with your goals.

Your cover letter needs to be well-written and succinct. You'll appear more professional if you use the standard business letter format, written in block style, left-justified text that's single-spaced with double spaces between paragraphs. Include the same contact information formatting as on the top of your resume and your documents will look like a matched set.

Write in a conversational tone, keeping your cover letter short and sweet. In most instances, 3-4 brief paragraphs will be most effective.

**Introductory paragraph:** Mention the position of interest and something specific you'll accomplish in the role. You can get this information from the job posting and the company's website. Include something that will differentiate you from other applicants.

**Body**: Employers will see right through a generic cover letter. In 1-2 paragraphs, explain how you'll add value to the organization and why you want to work specifically for their company. Customizing it with language they use on their website and in the posting will make you sound like you'll fit right in with their group. Include one relevant professional accomplishment (that appears on your resume) to demonstrate your qualifications. Be sure to connect the dots for the reader so they can see this achievement as proof that you have what they need.

---

**PRO TIP:** How you sign your cover letter is one way to let people know what you like to be called. For example, if your full name is William and you like to be called Will, you can sign your cover letter "Sincerely, Will."

---

**Closing paragraph:** Thank the employer for their time, reiterate why you're the ideal candidate for the role and request an interview. Conclude your letter with "Sincerely" or "Regards" and your name.

Typically, your cover letter is the first writing sample seen by a potential employer, so make sure yours will help, not hurt, your chances of winning an interview. Taking the time to write a strong letter and customizing it to each job for which you apply will help you impress employers. Make it intriguing so they'll want to meet you.

# SAMPLE COVER LETTER

**[Use the same heading as on your resume to make it a matched set]**

Date

Recipient Name
Recipient Title
Company Name
Mailing Address
City, State, Zip

Job Req. # (if provided)


Dear Recipient Name:

Mention the position for which you are applying and something specific you will accomplish in the role. You can get this information from the job posting. Include something interesting that differentiates you from other applicants.

Employers will see right through a generic cover letter. Customizing it with language they use on their website and in the job posting will make you sound like you'll fit right in with their group. Explain how you will add value to the organization and why you want to work specifically for their company.

Include one relevant professional accomplishment (that appears on your resume) to demonstrate your qualifications for the job. Be sure to connect the dots for the reader so they can see this achievement as proof that you have what they need.

Thank the employer for their time, reiterate why you are the ideal candidate for the role and request an interview.

Sincerely,

Your Preferred Name

# CHAPTER 7

# Acing Your Job Interview

nterviews can unnerve even the most experienced job seeker. And in today's competitive market, the hiring process has become even more complex. Experts agree that proper interview preparation can make the difference between landing the offer and being rejected. The key to interview success is to walk in with confidence rather than fear. You wouldn't ever show up for a big presentation without preparing your words and practicing your delivery, would you? A job interview requires the same level of attention. The way to do that is to prepare the way professional athletes do. Some rehearse until they get something right; others rehearse until they can't get it wrong. Then, give it all you have.

If you haven't interviewed in a while, you'll be surprised at how they've changed. Employers are asking candidates to jump through hoops and endure multiple rounds of interviews. Individual contributors (non-managers) are thrown into challenging workday scenarios, and executives are asked to present 30/60/90-day plans or complete "In Box Exercises" to demonstrate how they'll perform on the job. Interviewers are doing this to get past the canned answers to the most common and prepped-for questions so they can see the real candidate underneath.

If you've had many first-round job interviews but aren't invited back for a second, it may be time for some interview prep. Frequently the candidate who interviews best is the one who gets hired – not the most qualified or experienced. Your ability to communicate confidently can be as important to success on the job as the technical skills required. One of my recent clients, Sharon, was a brilliant data engineer but lacked self-confidence. She was so nervous during interviews that she couldn't sell herself well. We worked on composing impactful answers, finetuning in several rounds of edits, and then practiced with several mock interviews. We also created a library of situational success stories that demonstrated her leadership experience as well as her software coding, testing and troubleshooting expertise. Sharon aced her next rounds of interviews because the interviewers could see the immense value she offered the company. She was offered a great management role with a generous compensation package.

The interview is one of the most pivotal parts of a job search, yet many people fail to prepare properly. They don't like interviewing, so they don't want to practice. When your career is on the line, you can't just wing it. With a few hours of planning and preparation, you can be ready to sell yourself as the ideal candidate for the position. Composing answers to common interview questions is a great way to refine your messaging but don't focus too much on the questions themselves. Keep an eye on the bigger picture so you can show the hiring manager that you'd be an asset to their team. Your most effective approach is to develop situational stories that demonstrate your relevant qualifications and the depth of your experience. We'll get to sample questions and how to develop situational stories shortly.

## Different Interview Scenarios

The most common types of interviews are the initial telephone screening, the traditional in-person meeting between one candidate and one interviewer, the ever-intimidating panel interview, and the new recorded and live video interviews. Each has its own set of challenges and requires thorough preparation. While the mechanism may vary, every type of interview offers applicants the opportunity to impress their potential next boss. If a job seeker shows up unprepared, their candidacy is doomed from the start.

Frequently, hiring companies will pre-screen applicants with telephone interviews conducted by a recruiter or HR representative. These brief calls determine who will be selected for first-round interviews. Selling yourself well in a 5-minute phone conversation isn't easy. My #1 tip for mastering telephone interviews is to recognize that these are "real" interviews. Do your homework and be prepared to discuss the role and your salary requirements, but only if the interviewer mentions compensation first. You do not want to be the first person to bring up salary. If you're not comfortable speaking on the phone, start practicing now because it's a skill that can positively or negatively impact your professional career.

Schedule the call for a time when you'll be free to speak openly. If a recruiter calls with no warning, ask to call them right back as soon as you can move to a quieter spot — especially if you're at work. This will give you a moment to collect your thoughts. The best location is a private area with strong cell reception. Have the job posting, your resume, your cover letter and a list of questions to ask the interviewer available at your fingertips and make sure your phone battery is fully charged. Speak slowly and clearly, breathe deeply and don't ramble. And, of course, don't smoke, vape, chew gum or eat while on the phone. It can be helpful, however, to keep a glass of water handy just in case.

**PRO TIP:** Regardless of the role or industry, what a hiring manager really wants in an employee comes down to 3 things: someone who can do the job, who wants to do the job and who will fit in with their group. Focus on selling yourself in these 3 areas to set yourself apart from your competitors.

Be in the right frame of mind to succeed. Particularly when you don't have the benefit of seeing one another, you need to put energy into your voice to show that you're friendly, upbeat and interested in the job. Nod in agreement when the other person is speaking and smile when answering their questions. Your positive attitude will come through even though they can't see you. Stay in the moment. You can take notes while the interviewer is speaking as long as you can still concentrate on what's being said. As the interview comes to a close, thank the interviewer for their time. Let them know that you're looking forward to moving ahead in the interview process (if this is the case) and ask about the next steps. Immediately send a thank you email expressing your interest in the opportunity.

Digital technology has streamlined nearly every aspect of the hiring process. Virtual interviews are popular with employers because they can quickly help narrow the candidate pool, which saves the company time and money. But they can add an entirely new layer of anxiety for job seekers. Virtual interviews are becoming more commonplace due to the high availability of tech tools like Zoom, WebEx, Microsoft Teams, Skype and Facetime. You'll find that while most interviews are conducted via live video, more companies are starting to use Save & Record Interviews.

If you want to land that great new job, you must be prepared for video interviews. If you avoid them, you may be limiting your employment options. Because employers are increasingly relying on video interviews to evaluate candidates' soft skills, it's to your advantage to become comfortable with this type of interview. The good news about video interviews is that you can meet with recruiters and hiring managers from the comfort of your own home; the downside is that until you get used to interacting on camera, the interview process is even more nerve-wracking. Some people find virtual interviewing impersonal, but others find it makes the process less stressful. Keep in mind, even if you aren't meeting your interviewer in person, you still need to prepare your practice answers thoroughly and look the part.

Whether your video interview is live or recorded, the first thing you need to do is learn how to use the technology. A desktop or laptop computer with a webcam will look more professional than your phone. Choose a location that's comfortable, quiet and has a reliable internet connection. Avoid busy coffee shops, your car or windy outdoor locations. Declutter the room to eliminate any distracting objects in the background. Proper eye contact, lighting and camera angle will help you look your best.

In a recorded video interview, you're provided with a set of questions and you record your responses on camera. This approach can benefit both employers and job seekers, as it allows you to have a few practice runs before submitting your interview and HR doesn't have to coordinate scheduling between multiple parties. It can feel a little strange not to be face-to-face with your interviewer. The upside of these pre-recorded Q & A sessions is that you can listen to the questions and compose your answers before recording your response. Additionally, most systems let you watch your recording, delete and re-record your answers if you're not happy with your performance. This can be a real bonus for many nervous candidates. I, for one, have had in-person interviews where I wished I could turn back time.

If you don't already have it installed on your computer, you can easily download Zoom (the most popular platform) at no charge and set up a free user account. It's important that you use a professional-sounding username and a headshot for your profile. You don't want a silly username or selfie to negatively impact the hiring manager's first impression of you. Test and practice using the software a few days before your interview. Not only do you need to get comfortable with the software, but you also need to make sure that everything is working properly. You don't want to have a technical glitch in the middle of the interview! Ask a friend to run a practice session with you so you can identify and fix any potentially embarrassing problems. As you practice, position yourself so the other person can see you clearly. Check your lighting to make sure you're not backlit or in a spotlight.

On the day of the video interview, be sure to set up at least 10 minutes early. Remove any distractions and post a "Do Not

Disturb" sign if you're not alone. It can be difficult to recover from an interruption. Dress and groom to impress. Remember, this is a real interview, and you must look professional. Even though you should expect to be seated during the entire interview, please don't wear sweatpants with your suit jacket. You don't want to be distracted. ("Hmmm... I wonder if they can tell?")

While you can't shake the interviewer's hand in a video interview, you can nod, smile and say their name as you introduce yourself. This serves as a "virtual handshake." It may feel awkward but concentrate on looking directly into the camera to establish natural eye contact. To avoid looking down at your papers, you may find it helpful to tape your speaking points right next to your camera.

Your body language, facial expressions and overall appearance convey more information than your words, so sit up straight and try not to fidget. Many hiring managers say they're put off by a candidate who has bad posture because they look disinterested. Even small movements like clenching your fists, tapping your fingers or bouncing your leg can be emphasized on camera. Breathe normally, speak clearly and enunciate. Speak a little louder and slower than you normally would. When asked a question, pause, think, then answer succinctly.

In-person interviews had started to diminish even before the COVID-19 pandemic made face-to-face interactions dangerous. Skyrocketing travel costs and geographically dispersed teams prompted many companies to interview candidates virtually using video conferencing. But in-office interviews are still the norm for most organizations with a physical location.

When invited to an employer's office for a job interview, start things off right by arriving on time. Obtain driving directions and parking details a few days in advance and leave 20 to 30 minutes earlier than you think you should. You'll want to enter the building 5 to 7 minutes before your scheduled appointment. This gives you time to catch your breath, familiarize yourself with the name of the person with whom you're meeting and reread the job posting. If you arrive at your location early, wait in your car. A quick review of your resume is a terrific way to boost your confidence.

Your interview actually begins as soon as you enter the parking lot. Don't cut someone off to grab the last parking space. You never know if that person could be your interviewer or have an influence on the hiring decision. Be courteous to everyone you meet and observant of your surroundings. Does the office have a professional atmosphere? Do the people look happy? Is this somewhere you might like to work? Announce yourself politely to the receptionist and follow their instructions. If you have a few minutes to wait, stay patiently seated without looking at your phone, which should already be turned off. Take a few deep breaths, put a smile on your face and wait for your opportunity to shine.

Here are some tips to help you ace the interview itself, based upon the biggest pet peeves I hear from recruiters and hiring managers.

- **Don't be late.** No matter the reason, if you can't get to the interview on time, you may be seen as unreliable. If a real emergency is preventing your timely arrival, you should call to explain your situation before the interview start time.

- **Ditch your cell phone.** Either turn it off and keep it in your pocket or leave it in the car. It's common courtesy. Don't just turn the volume down or mute it. Turn it completely off. And please don't put it on the table — that will just distract you both. Nothing is more annoying to a hiring manager, who is taking valuable time out of their busy day to talk to you, than cell phone interruptions. Hopefully, they'll have theirs turned off and out of sight as well.

‣ **Be polite.** Studies have shown that you have 5 seconds to make a first impression. Your manners, or lack thereof, can either impress the interviewer or disqualify you from consideration. These tips pertain more to in-person interviews but are good to keep in mind for any business meeting. When you enter the interview room, don't sit down before being offered a chair. Stand until you're invited to sit or politely ask where you should sit. And if you're seated when the interviewer enters, you should stand up to greet them.

‣ **Be ready to win them over.** Lack of interview preparation implies that you aren't serious about the job. Don't assume that because you uploaded your resume with your online application that the interviewer will have it on hand. People get busy, forget to print things out and, let's face it, interviewing you isn't the only thing on their to-do list. You may be interviewing with several people, so it's advisable to bring 3 to 4 copies of your resume printed on nice paper to show that you're thorough and well organized.

‣ **Do your research.** This should be obvious, but hiring managers complain that many candidates show up to the interview without knowing a thing about the company or the role. Interviewers expect you to have done your homework.

Before the interview, review the company's website to learn about its history, products and management team. That way, when the interviewer asks you, "What interests you about this role?" or "Why exactly do you want to work here?" you'll have several good reasons ready to share.

➲ **A proper handshake shows that you're a confident person with good social skills.** Not only does it set the tone for the interview, but your handshake can also leave a lasting impression. Make sure yours conveys professionalism and sincerity. A bone-crushing grip can make you look like you're trying too hard, while a limp handshake can make you appear timid. Please pardon these gender stereotypes, but women need to avoid the "boneless" or "fingertips only" handshakes and offer a firm handshake. And men, please don't be afraid to shake a woman's hand. She won't break!

**PRO TIP:** The key to the perfect handshake? Make solid palm-to-palm contact where the webbing between your thumb and first finger meets that of the other person. Know when to let go! The ideal handshake lasts about three seconds. Gently pump your hand three or four times, then pull back. Make and hold eye contact with the other person and don't forget to smile.

➲ **Be attentive and present.** During the interview, maintain steady eye contact. You might find it easier to soften your gaze by focusing on the interviewer's entire face. Try not to look down or let your eyes drift around the room. Do your best not to interrupt your interviewer and answer their questions clearly and concisely. Don't ramble, which can cause the listener to tune out.

➲ **Follow up every time.** Your interview doesn't end when you leave the meeting or video call. Managers like proactive and ambitious employees, and many dismiss candidates who don't follow up after the interview. It's an easy way for them to weed out the weakest candidates. It's considerate and expected to immediately send a handwritten note or email (both would be great!) thanking the interviewer for taking the time to meet with you. Don't miss this opportunity to remind the interviewer of your qualifications and add significant details that didn't come up during the interview. Make yourself memorable.

Follow up, per the timeframe agreed upon with the interviewer. If you don't hear back, reaching out a week later with an invitation to connect on LinkedIn is a great soft touch reminder that will keep you "top of mind." Sitting around waiting for a callback is a big mistake. No matter how well you feel the interview went, you need to continue pursuing other job leads.

➲ **Be prepared to ask your own questions.** In addition to being ready to answer the interviewer's questions, they'll expect you to have several of your own to ask. Insightful questions can show that you're eager about the role. Open-ended questions are best because they encourage conversation flow.

In addition to role-specific questions for areas needing clarification, I recommend you ask thoughtful, future-focused questions like, "What do you see in the marketplace right now?", "Where do you think the industry is headed?" and "What do you think is the biggest upcoming challenge for the organization?" Another benefit to having a list of questions ready is that during an awkward pause, asking a question will subtly turn the attention away from you.

**Be careful.** Asking the wrong type of questions can make you look self-serving and could cost you the job. No matter how curious you are, don't ask about compensation, paid time off, tuition reimbursement, benefits or raise timelines. If the interviewer does mention salary or benefits, consider the topic open for discussion.

## Interview Prep – Conquer the Fear!

There's no way around it. Interview preparation is critical to your success. Regardless of how high up the ladder you have climbed so far, you need to be ready to answer skills-based, situational and behavioral questions. Because you never know how long the interview will last or which questions you may be asked, it's best to work your strengths and expertise into every answer. Show the employer that you offer a valuable skillset that they need on their team.

**PRO TIP:** Interview questions tend to fall into 3 general buckets: icebreakers, job-specific qualifications and behavioral competencies like your ability to adapt, communicate, work on a team, resolve conflict and make a decision.

Some interviewers use small talk at the beginning of the conversation to put you at ease or to see how you act when you let your guard down. They may start the interview with the seemingly innocuous "So, tell me about yourself…" This is actually a loaded question that most unprepared candidates answer completely wrong and hurt their candidacy. There are many things that employers aren't allowed by law to ask applicants but would like to know. To make the best hiring decision, they want to know if there's anything in your personal life that would prevent you from being the ideal employee. Young children at home, caring for aging parents, family problems or health concerns might compete for your time and attention. The interviewer may be curious about your age, ethnicity, religion or relationship status but can't inquire. When asked this simple open-ended question, many job seekers divulge personal information that they should keep to themselves.

You want to answer this question by introducing the professional you and playing up your strengths that relate to the job. Don't worry; you don't have to start from scratch. Go back to the Compelling Conversation Opener you developed a few chapters ago. Expand upon that and relate it to the role for which you're interviewing. Maybe add some information from the summary section of your resume. Keep it short and upbeat: 3 to 4 sentences should suffice. Make it interesting to jumpstart the conversation.

Here's a simple formula for winning interview answers: start off with something positive, answer the question, then wrap up with another positive statement. For example, if you're asked about your leadership style, you could answer, "I take pride in the highly engaged teams I've built through my inclusive leadership style. I've learned over the years that I can get the most out of my teams by being transparent, honest and clearly outlining objectives. My staff knows I have their back and they have mine."

If you're explaining something negative, like a mistake you've made, the positive bookends are even more important. "Yes, I am human and do occasionally make mistakes, but I do my best to learn from them, so they're never repeated. There once was a project where we missed a deadline because I didn't keep my eye on the ball. The client was upset, as were our senior leaders, and rightly so. As soon as I became aware of the problem, I addressed it directly with all stakeholders, sincerely apologized and immediately rectified it. Since then, I've never missed a deadline because I use a project planning spreadsheet to track progress and due dates for deliverables." This approach of showing how you overcame a shortcoming can also be used to explain why any weakness you may have won't impact your ability to do the job. Hiring managers like employees who are self-aware and continually trying to improve themselves. Make sure you don't share a serious mistake that you can't speak about without emotion. Pick one that you can discuss calmly and wrap up in a positive manner.

Two things you want to avoid saying in an interview are "No" and "I don't know." As soon as someone hears the word "No," they tend to stop listening. But, at the same time, you do need to be honest. So, if the interviewer asks you if you have a certain type of experience and you don't, a good answer might be something like, "That's quite similar to what I did at X. While somewhat different…" and draw some similarities between the challenges or your approach. If you're asked a question you can't answer, you could say, "Hmm, I've never thought about that. Let me think about that for a moment." Many people will appreciate your candor and desire to answer thoughtfully.

Add impact to your answers with relevant examples that demonstrate how previous employers benefited from you doing your job so well. Situational stories are considered performance indicators, so many interviewers will ask, "Tell me about a time when…" Use quantified and qualified achievements from throughout your career to build C-A-R (Challenge, Action and Result) stories. Include both hard skills and the more subjective soft skills in every story, emphasizing the qualifications that enable you to excel in your role. Your resume should be full of specific examples of how you added value to an organization. Expand upon some of those in an interview to demonstrate the depth of your expertise.

Develop 6 to 8 examples that can address multiple situational questions. For instance, a story about a significant problem you resolved might also showcase your decision-making and influencing abilities. Keep the stories short and focused at no more than 3 to 4 sentences each. The interviewer can always ask follow-up questions if they'd like more details.

Putting time and effort into preparing what you'd like to say will pay off during the interview. Write out your answers in a conversational tone, so they don't sound completely scripted. I like to begin some sentences with transitional phrases (however, as a result, meanwhile, furthermore, after all, even so, in addition, on the other hand, for example) for smooth cadence. After you've composed your answers, go through a few rounds of revisions to improve the wording even further. Rehearse by reading your answers out loud, continuing until you've memorized your answers and can speak the words comfortably. The next step is to ask someone to do a mock interview so you can practice in front of another person. Now, onto some sample questions to help you prepare.

## Sample Interview Questions

In addition to determining your role-specific qualifications, employers may ask behavioral questions to learn about your soft skills, including your work ethic, communication style, ability to adapt, solve a problem, work on a team, resolve conflict, own up to a mistake and make decisions. Their wording may vary, but these are the types of questions you can expect to be asked.

1. What are you the proudest of? (Can be personal or professional)

2. What do you do to relax / for fun outside of work?

3. Tell me about a blog or book you've read recently.

4. Please describe for me your 3 greatest strengths.

5. What types of things do you find challenging? (Similar to your weaknesses)

6. Describe a rewarding day on the job.

7. Why are you leaving X company / X industry?

8. What would previous managers / co-workers say about you?

9. Where do you see yourself in 5 years? 10 years?

10. What interests you most about this role?

11. How do you manage your time and stay on top of multiple priorities?

12. How would you characterize your ability to collaborate / get along with colleagues?

13. How do you feel you've contributed to the success of your previous employers?

14. Describe your approach to problem-solving.

15. Where do you naturally fall on a team?

16. Share with me a time when you had a difficult co-worker or boss.

17. Tell me about a time when you made a mistake. What happened and how did you improve the situation?

18. Did you ever have to overcome a major obstacle to complete a project?

19. Describe a situation in which you've experienced a significant change that you weren't expecting. How did that impact you and how did you adapt to this change?

20. I'd be interested in hearing about a miscommunication you had with a supervisor. What was the reason for that? How did you resolve it?

21. Tell me about when you had to deal with conflict within your team. How was the conflict resolved? What did you learn from the situation?

22. Think about a time when you made a poor decision, or something just didn't turn out right. What happened? Would you do anything differently today?

23. Describe a situation in which you had difficulty getting others to accept your ideas. What was your approach? Were you able to persuade them to see things your way?

24. Give me a recent example of a stressful situation on the job. What happened? How did you handle it?

25. Why should I hire you over other candidates? What differentiates you from the rest?

# CHAPTER 8

# Roadmap to Success

Job hunting these days is not for the unprepared or faint of heart. Many experienced professionals are surprised that they can't just casually step back into a job search and be successful. The job market is crowded and super competitive because digital platforms like LinkedIn have expanded the candidate pool. To gain an employer's attention in our highly connected world, you need to rise above the online noise to stand out among your competitors. Drawing from my experience helping hundreds of people conduct successful job searches and my training in current hiring practices, here are 2 insights into the digital job search that I encourage you to embrace:

❶ Job search success depends upon your ability to articulate your personal brand.

❷ Networking is crucial for people in every type of role and at every level.

Because many companies don't want to risk hiring a stranger, they only post jobs internally and ask for employee referrals. Strategic networking can provide you access to these internal postings before anyone else even knows about them — especially at the senior leadership level. So why do so many job seekers spend countless hours in front of their computer combing through online job boards? Because they're using job search techniques that served them well in previous job searches. That was then; this is now. Today's digital job search is a new playing field where outdated strategies simply aren't as effective.

I find that for many of the executives who come to me after a failed job search, it's their long-held beliefs that are holding them back. They're resistant to change and clinging to old ways of doing things. As soon as they agree to try my suggested methods, which are based on current best practices, their job searches start gaining traction. While there's no magic wand, my techniques have worked for multitudes of people, many in situations just like yours. I highly recommend the 80/20 rule: spend 80% of your time actively looking for work through networking and only 20% passively searching online.

The concept of networking your way to a job is new to many people, but industry statistics show that it's the most effective way to land a new job. If you want to move up in your career or land a role at a new company, you're going to have to put yourself out there. Networking itself is not new; it's just labeled now. It's relationship building. Online platforms like LinkedIn make it even easier to reach out and engage with your professional peers so you can build a wide group of contacts who know you, like and trust you.

## Create Your Target Company List

You don't want just any job. You want the right job for you. You previously determined your desired job title, characteristics of the role, the type of company, geography and salary range. Great! Now, where are the jobs?

They're right there waiting for you, but you must be proactive and get in front of the decision-makers. The first step is to identify the companies where you'll be most marketable. This preliminary information gathering lays the foundation for your successful job search.

Online search engines make company research easier than ever before. To build your target list, use Google to identify the appropriate companies in your targeted geographic area. Ask industry connections, people you know (or meet) about where they work or companies they've heard positive things about. For more general employer research, state government websites have free online databases of registered businesses and the US Department of Labor's CareerOneStop offers a free searchable company database in its Toolkit section. Additionally, many library cardholders can access free research tools like Reference Solutions (formerly ReferenceUSA) and Plunkett Research Online through their local library's website. These databases let you search by industry, company name, location, financial information, number of employees and other qualifying details.

Once you have a list of 25 to 30 potential employers, learn as much as you can about them from multiple sources. Visit each company's website to determine if it's an organization where you might like to work. Read their annual reports and what others have to say about them in the news, trade publications and employee testimonials. Glassdoor and LinkedIn are great resources to help you decide if a company is a good fit for you personally and professionally. Glassdoor employee reviews are helpful but keep in mind that happy people tend not to post about their employers as often as disgruntled ones. It can be beneficial to speak directly with current and former employees to find out the true company culture and what it's really like to work there. Use LinkedIn to search for a company's former or current employees in roles similar to yours and ask them for 5 minutes of their time to chat about their personal experiences. I've found most LinkedIn members to be very friendly and helpful.

Narrow your list to 10 to 15 target companies you admire, who need employees with your skillset and tend to pay within your desired salary range. Payscale.com is a great resource to determine your salary range, factoring in your geographic area and level of experience. Don't let a lack of posted job openings deter you. If you happen to see an appropriate posting on a company's website, fantastic! Apply away! Because many employers don't post jobs externally until they've exhausted their internal and network referral resources, they still may have an opening in their team. Research the management team to identify the individual who might be the hiring manager for your type of role. Obtain their name and contact information so you can reach out, add them to your professional network and start building a relationship.

**PRO TIP:** An active job search centers on establishing your professional brand beyond your immediate sphere of influence through face-to-face and online networking.

## Your Job Search Plan

Now that you know where you want to work and have a strong career marketing portfolio (CCO, resume, cover letter and LinkedIn profile), the next challenge is to map out a step-by-step job search plan. Job searches can be overwhelming, especially if you haven't done one in a while. Focusing your search with a structured plan and the right effort can get you into your next job sooner. This list may seem long, but your daily plan will break it down into manageable tasks. That will help you stay on track and the logical sequence will keep you moving forward.

Important job search tasks:

- Stay up on news in your industry and current initiatives at your target companies.

- Consider every person a potential recommendation, job lead or referral source.

- Reach out directly to potential hiring managers (Not HR unless you've applied for a posted job) via email, phone or LinkedIn messaging.

- Schedule career research conversations and informal coffee meetings. You can ask about their career journey or thoughts on the industry but don't directly ask for a job.

- Introduce yourself to recruiters who specialize in your industry.

- Reconnect with industry connections, former managers, colleagues and clients.

- Expand your LinkedIn connections and engage in conversations.

- Earn credibility by posting, commenting and re-sharing relevant content on LinkedIn.

- Continue with your interview prep and reciting your CCO out loud.

- To maintain your marketability, take training to keep your skills sharp or gain new ones.

- Request warm introductions to decision-makers at your target companies.

- Apply online for appropriate jobs as you see them.

- For networking purposes, order business cards that highlight your target industries and areas of expertise.

- Attend in-person and virtual networking events, making sure to follow up with new acquaintances.

- Prepare your interview outfit, buy an attractive portfolio and order some nice resume paper.

I encourage you to set a realistic goal regarding how much you can accomplish per day. Set up your daily task list according to the number of hours you believe you'll honestly spend on your job search. Maintaining a Monday through Friday schedule and assigning a variety of tasks to each day will remind you not to neglect any one aspect of your job search. For example, you shouldn't spend so much of your time on LinkedIn or researching companies that it comes at the expense of interview prep. A consistent approach to expanding your brand awareness will help you get in front of decision-makers at your target companies. This increased visibility will also draw the attention of recruiters sourcing talent, so the right opportunity just might find you.

I like to use Microsoft Excel spreadsheets for the daily planner and to organize job search activities. You can lay out your daily tasks on one tab.

| DAY | TASK | DONE |
|---|---|---|
| MONDAY | Identify decision-makers at target companies. | ___ |
| | Check for posted job opening or news briefs on target company websites | ___ |
| | Set up a job seeker account on a target company website | ___ |
| | Send a LinkedIn message to 3 friends or people you used to work with | ___ |
| | Read/share/comment on LinkedIn news/post pertaining to your role/industry | ___ |
| TUESDAY | Share a post of interest on LinkedIn/comment on another's post | ___ |
| | Customize your LinkedIn newsfeed, follow hashtags of interest | ___ |
| | Schedule coffee date or Zoom call with an industry connection | ___ |
| | Engage in LinkedIn cooooonversations | ___ |
| | Follow companies of interest  on LinkedIn. | ___ |
| WEDNESDAY | Send an introductory email to 1 new LinkedIn connection | ___ |
| | Research and subscribe to an industry newsletter and blog | ___ |
| | Add more companies to target list if necessary. Identify decisionmakers. | ___ |
| | Visit a target company's LinkedIn page, comment on/reshare their post | ___ |
| | Schedule a coffee date or Zoom call with one of your industry connections | ___ |
| THURSDAY | Send intro email to 2 targeted decisionmakers with resume attached | ___ |
| | Search online for any in-person networking events in your area | ___ |
| | Visit decisionmakers' profiles and comment on their posts | ___ |
| | Share a post of interest on LinkedIn/comment on another's post | ___ |
| FRIDAY | Add one skill, course or new keyword to your LinkedIn profile | ___ |
| | Ask 2 recruiters to connect on LinkedIn with a customized message | ___ |
| | Search/apply for jobs on LinkedIn. Record on 4th tab of spreadsheet | ___ |
| | Review colleagues' LinkedIn connections to ID who to connect with | ___ |
| | Ask 4 people to connect on LinkedIn with a customized message | ___ |
| SATURDAY | Relax | ___ |
| SUNDAY | Take a quick online training class/webinar pertaining to your next role | ___ |
| | Catch up on steps not completed earlier in the week | ___ |

Manage all your target company contacts in one place.

| TARGET COMPANY LIST | | | | | |
|---|---|---|---|---|---|
| Company | Location | Website | Contact Name / Title | Email | Telephone |
| ABC, Inc. | Avon, CT | www.abcinc.com | Jane Doe / Chief Marketing Officer | jane.doe@abcinc.com | 123-456-7890 |
| XYZ Company | Farmington, CT | www.xyz-co.com | John Q. Public / Director, Int'l Marketing | jqpublic@xyz-co.com | 456-789-0101 |

Logging jobs you have applied for, interviews, meetings, networking events and significant connections will help you keep track of contact information and due dates.

| | | | | JOB SEARCH EFFORTS | | | | |
|---|---|---|---|---|---|---|---|---|
| Date | Company / Event | Job of Interest | Contact | Email | Phone | Activity | Next Steps | Notes |
| | | | | | | | | |
| | | | | | | | | |
| | | | | | | | | |
| | | | | | | | | |
| | | | | | | | | |
| | | | | | | | | |
| | | | | | | | | |
| | | | | | | | | |
| | | | | | | | | |
| | | | | | | | | |
| | | | | | | | | |
| | | | | | | | | |

# CHAPTER 9

# Tips to Improve Your Job Search

## Networking

Networking doesn't have to be scary. It's just two people interacting, discussing a topic of mutual interest. Sometimes this takes place in a room full of many people doing the same thing; other times, it's a one-on-one conversation in a quiet coffee shop. Choose the scenario that works best for you. I'm somewhat outgoing but truly an introvert who finds large events extremely draining. I'm not the social butterfly who works the room and casually speaks to everyone. Extroverts thrive in this type of environment and get energized by groups of people. I prefer to have fewer conversations where I can actually get to know someone. Honoring my inner introvert, I gear myself up psychologically before a large event or speaking engagement and then schedule quiet time afterward to recharge my batteries.

There are a few things you can do pre- and post-event to leverage the benefits of networking. If you preregistered for the event, review the attendee list in advance to familiarize yourself with key names. You can even reach out to a few people on LinkedIn and arrange to meet up at the event. Reviewing their profile can provide conversation fodder and identify any mutual acquaintances. At the event, collect business cards from anyone with whom you'd like to follow up and then send them an invitation to connect on LinkedIn so you can continue the conversation. Don't worry if they're not in your industry. I encourage you to consider every person a potential job lead or source of inspiration.

A few tips to make networking at an event easier for you:

- Practice saying your CCO aloud, so you'll be prepared to introduce yourself.

- Don't put pressure on yourself to meet "the right person" or come out of the event with a meeting scheduled. Just attend the event with an open mind.

- Set yourself up for success with a reasonable goal of introducing yourself to 3 people.

- Ask someone about themselves before launching into CCO mode. Keeping the conversation light, you could ask about a book they enjoyed or something interesting they accomplished this week.

- Rescue someone who's looking lost in the corner of the room.

Generosity and being able to start a conversation with a stranger are qualities that will take you far in life. Networking is something you should do throughout your career, not just during your job search. Stay in touch with your professional network — don't just reach out to ask for a favor. Nurture your relationships as you would a garden and you'll build a strong network of allies. People who know, like and trust you are the most effective job search tool. If you've neglected your professional network in recent years,

LinkedIn can help you reconnect. Its notification feature alerts you to your connections' birthdays, work anniversaries and new jobs. These are all natural opportunities to reach out to someone you haven't spoken to for a while.

## References and Recommendations

As you advance through the hiring process, chances are HR will ask you for your references or letters of recommendation. Actual written letters of recommendation are considered outdated, but some companies and state job applications still require them. Generally, these have been replaced by the LinkedIn recommendation. The only drawback there is that the person writing the recommendation must also be a LinkedIn member. Because obtaining references and written recommendations can take some time, you may want to send your requests early. Make sure you ask people who will, in fact, say nice things about you. If you're not sure, you can ask them what they plan to say, or suggest a specific skill or quality you'd like them to mention. If you didn't leave on good terms with a previous manager, maybe one of their peers or their manager would vouch for you. One of the greatest things about LinkedIn is that your contact list is always up to date. Even if a former colleague has moved on, you have their contact information if they've kept their profile current.

## Working With Recruiters

How to connect with recruiters is one of the most frequent questions I hear from my clients. If you're considering reaching out to a recruiter for help landing a job, you first need to understand how recruiters work and where they might fit in your job search.

It's important to note that you, the job seeker, are generally not the recruiter's client. Apart from certain executive search firms, recruiters work for the employer vs. a career coach who does work for you and has your best interests at heart.

**There are three primary types of recruiters (all paid by the employer, not individual job seekers):**

➲ Internal company recruiters who fill the candidate pipeline for their own employer.

➲ Agency or contingency recruiters who work for themselves and are contracted by employers to fill specific roles.

➲ Staffing agency recruiters who are paid a fee by their company clients for a successful temporary or permanent placement.

Companies pay recruiters to fill their open positions with candidates who have the exact qualifications the employer requires and will be the right cultural fit. That means a recruiter won't find you a job. You must do that part by yourself. When you hear about people "working with headhunters," in reality, the recruiter is assisting the employer, not the job seeker. If the individual is a perfect fit for a specific role the recruiter is trying to fill at just that moment, great! They may present the candidate to the client. But the recruiter truly works for the employer, and that's whose interests they value.

I'm not saying don't include recruiters in your overall job search strategy. I just want you to have realistic expectations. Because they're the conduit between you and the company, experienced recruiters who know the job market and are well-connected in your industry can be a valuable resource. The most effective approach is to build friendly relationships with recruiters in your industry and make sure they know the value you offer an organization. Online networking is the best way to do that.

According to Jobvite's 2020 Recruiter Nation Survey, 72% of recruiters report using LinkedIn for recruitment. They're searching for candidates who exactly match their client's requirements. You can become a recruiter magnet by optimizing your LinkedIn profile with the keywords that show your qualifications match their open roles. You can use LinkedIn's Open to Work feature to notify recruiters that you're available, but I don't recommend letting everyone know that you're out of work by putting the green "Open to Work" frame around your headshot. Isn't your expertise more important than the fact that you're in transition?

You can also proactively invite recruiters to connect on LinkedIn. But first, do your research to identify recruiters who actually fill your type of role in your industry. If you want to be taken seriously, send a personalized note to each person, not a canned message. Even if it's well written, a generic message is a big turn-off. Make it easy for a recruiter to contact you by including your telephone number and email address at the end of your profile's About section. As of this writing, you can't include any kind of link within invitations to connect, but I believe you can attach your resume to an InMail. Personally, I won't pay for InMails. I find workarounds to contact anyone I need to for free, and you can too. Be friendly, introduce yourself and start a conversation. Just like in other aspects of your life, relationship building is important.

## Decoding Job Descriptions

Learning how to read a job description is a critical skill for job seekers at every level because it helps you determine if the job is right for you. It also enables you to tailor your application support materials: your resume, cover letter and even your LinkedIn profile. Unfortunately, not all job postings are well written. Sometimes they're created by the hiring manager who knows the job but not how to put the information into proper HR jargon. Other times, the HR representative is given minimal information to go on. This is another instance when reaching out to a current or former employee on LinkedIn might be extremely helpful.

To make sure you're a good fit for the job and that the job is a good fit for you, you need to read the posting carefully and completely. Considering the role's responsibilities and qualifications, honestly evaluate your ability and desire to do the job. I'm a visual person, so when I review a job posting, I highlight the matching skills in one color and the skills my client lacks in another. Sometimes postings are so brief that they barely describe the qualifications the employer is looking for. That's when researching other job postings on the company's website, especially if there's one for the role to which this position reports, can help. I also review postings for similar roles at other companies to gather more information. And don't discount your own professional knowledge. If you've been in the field for a while, you know the skills required and your suitability.

To determine proper fit, focus on the qualifications that are *required* for the role rather than those listed as *preferred*. If you don't have most of the required qualifications, accept that this may not be the right job for you. And that's okay. Not every job will be a good fit for what you offer an organization. Applying for long-shot jobs may not be the best use of your time. Stretch roles, where you meet at least 70% of the requirements, can sometimes pan out if you have an in with the company. That's the beauty of networking — the personal approach can give you a leg up. But when applying online, you'll be competing with candidates who meet 100% of the role's requirements, which will make it harder for you to win an interview.

**PRO TIP:** One of the best job postings I've ever read, and I've read thousands, included this request: *"Please be crystal clear when describing your skills and qualifications. We don't know what you can do until you tell us."* That is brilliant!

Advanced degrees and years of experience are typically not negotiable items as they indicate the level of expertise the job demands. But it really comes down to having the required knowledge. This is where recent professional development courses and micro-certifications can strengthen your candidacy. Because experience is more valuable than a decades-old college degree, the longer you're in a field, the more forgiving a company tends to be on required degrees. More than anything, the employer wants to know that you have the ability to excel on the job. Early in your career, that knowledge comes through formal education; once you've been in the role a while, you've developed valuable institutional knowledge.

Employers across industries are reporting a frustrating skills mismatch, which is why so many people are unemployed while positions remain unfilled. There's an easy remedy to this, job seekers! When you're reading job postings and you notice they're asking for skills and qualifications you don't have focus on learning them. There are plenty of self-paced training opportunities available for almost any technical skill — many at no charge. Enrolling in some free or inexpensive training for the most in-demand skills can help you land your next job sooner. As soon as the training is complete, add it to your resume, cover letter and LinkedIn profile so employers know you have the qualifications they need. Then, highlight your newly gained education when you apply for jobs. Prospective employers will be impressed that you continue to grow professionally.

## Online Job Applications

I frequently hear from job seekers how time-consuming the online job application process is and how aggravating it can be to submit dozens of online job applications and never receive a response. They wonder if their resume even made it through the Applicant Tracking System — a legitimate concern.

Because of the tight job market, you need to work even harder to gain the competitive edge over other candidates. When completing an application, it's crucial that you answer every question as well as possible, making sure your spelling, grammar and punctuation are perfect. This is made more difficult by the fact that the input fields you type into are so small that you can barely see what you're typing. Many of these online application systems don't even have a spellcheck feature. One typo, and you're out of the running.

---

**PRO TIP:** Microsoft Word can help increase the quality of your online job applications and reduce the time it takes to apply.

---

Because these online application systems are notorious for freezing up and timing out due to the high volume of incoming resumes, you need to save your work frequently. This can disrupt your train of thought, which only adds to the anxiety of answering the application questions well.

Here's a tip that can speed up completing online job applications as well as help you to increase the quality of your applications: Copy the questions from the online system into a Microsoft Word document and then compose your answers to the questions in Word. Refine and edit your answers until they shine. Use Microsoft's spelling and grammar check and word count features to fine-tune your responses and stay within the field constraints. When you're satisfied with your answers, copy and paste them into the appropriate fields of the online application. Then, save that Word document.

Because many companies ask similar questions about how the position is a good match for your skillset, etc., you can use that document as a starting point for your next application. After doing this a few times, you'll have a library of good, strong answers that should only need minor tweaking for future job applications. This technique can reduce the time it takes to complete an online application from an hour to about 15 minutes. And the quality of your submissions should improve as well.

Make sure you answer every question thoroughly, as many companies use incomplete applications to weed out candidates. Although the answer to a question may appear unnecessary because the information appears somewhere on your resume, if you respond, "see resume," you will probably be seen as lazy and not be selected for an interview. Some applicants skip over the salary question because they don't want to be eliminated with a figure that's outside of the salary range. But failing to answer it can have the same negative result. Research the average salary for your role in your geographic area and then enter a valid salary within that range that you would be satisfied with earning.

## Overcoming Employment Obstacles

Discrimination and unconscious bias can impede your job search and overall career success, but they're not insurmountable. The key is to understand and proactively neutralize employer concerns. Keep in mind that recruiters and hiring managers are people too, and we all have preconceived ideas and expectations (both good and bad) based upon previous experiences. Here are a few tips to overcoming the most prevalent employer biases throughout the hiring process, specifically on your resume and in a job interview.

Age discrimination is the most commonly reported hiring bias among job seekers aged 50+, but I've found that many times it's an incorrect assumption on the part of the job seeker. In reality, they were using outdated job search tactics or simply weren't selling themselves as highly valuable candidates.

Make sure your resume is age-neutral, so the reader sees you only as having a valuable skillset they need on their team. When you use a modern Applicant Tracking System-compatible resume format, don't include any employment or education dates prior to 2000 and omit any outdated technology, your age shouldn't even be a factor. If an employer is truly questioning your ability to do the job because of your higher age, you can frequently counteract their bias by showing them that you're at your prime with high energy, a future-focused outlook and strong tech skills.

## Employment obstacles include:

➲ Over the age of 50

➲ Overqualified

➲ Employment gaps

➲ Excessive job jumping

➲ Limited work experience

➲ Mid-career reinvention

➲ Re-entering the paid workforce

➲ Lack of training or education

➲ Criminal offenses / serious career mistakes

Reality check: none of us are perfect! You decide what information goes on your resume. While always being honest, include only your best material and what's relevant to this next chapter in your career. Make it easy for the reader to see that you have a lot to offer them. Highlight your strengths to downplay any shortcomings. For instance, if you have a spotty career record, you can impress the reader with your summary section and areas of expertise before they even get to your professional experience section and see your employment history.

Here are some suggestions for overcoming some of the more common employer biases.

## AGEISM

| THEIR CONCERN | HOW TO OVERCOME IT |
|---|---|
| • Poor tech skills<br>• Resistance to change<br>• Not wanting to work with younger people<br>• Looking to coast at end of career<br>• Low energy / failing health<br>• Caring for aging parents | • Mention software you use, online courses taken, inter-generational experience and how you adapted well to COVID-related changes<br>• Share what you'd like to accomplish next<br>• Play up physically active hobbies<br>• Don't mention health or family, period |

## OVERQUALIFIED

| THEIR CONCERN | HOW TO OVERCOME IT |
|---|---|
| • High salary requirements<br>• Superior attitude<br>• May get bored in lower-level job<br>• Filler job, will leave for better role<br>• Afraid you'll take their job | • Do research and clarify your expectations<br>• Downplay leadership responsibilities, higher titles<br>• Proactively explain your motivation<br>• Reassure them that you really want this job and plan to stay |

## EMPLOYMENT GAPS OR JOB JUMPING

| THEIR CONCERN | HOW TO OVERCOME IT |
|---|---|
| • Get bored / give up easily Fired for poor performance<br>• Don't have skills claimed | • Omit months in dates on resume<br>• Fill gaps with volunteer work or education<br>• Explain if laid off, not fired |

## LACK OF TRAINING OR FORMAL EDUCATION

| THEIR CONCERN | HOW TO OVERCOME IT |
|---|---|
| • Outdated skills<br>• Mediocre performance<br>• Don't care about personal growth<br>• If < 30, lack of maturity, can't commit to a goal | • Take some online courses now!<br>• Include self-study, workshops, CE credits, industry conferences<br>• List college coursework you have taken even if you didn't graduate |

## MISTAKES IN YOUR PAST

**THEIR CONCERN**
- Bad personal decisions = bad work decisions
- Might make the same mistake again
- May put company at risk

**HOW TO OVERCOME IT**
- Don't include it on your resume
- In the interview, briefly explain without emotion, stick to facts, don't blame others. Share what you learned from it and that it won't happen again
- Let go of the mistake, retain the lesson
- Move on to next topic

## MID-CAREER REINVENTION

**THEIR CONCERN**
- Won't have the skills to do the job
- Longer learning curve
- Wants to work at a slower pace

**HOW TO OVERCOME IT**
- Emphasize similarities between roles / industries
- Explain the benefits of diverse experience
- Share your enthusiasm for changing careers

## LIMITED WORK EXPERIENCE

**THEIR CONCERN**
- Won't know business protocol, reporting structure, email etiquette
- Unprofessional conduct
- Need more onboarding support
- Longer learning curve / more mistakes
- Poor communication skills

**HOW TO OVERCOME IT**
- Emphasize similar skills used in school
- Share eagerness to assimilate quickly
- Play up strengths, maturity, enthusiasm, potential
- Ask questions to clarify expectations
- Don't ever use texting abbreviations or emojis

## RE-ENTERING PAID WORKFORCE

**THEIR CONCERN**
- Outdated skills
- Longer learning curve
- Can't handle the stress
- Distracted by personal commitments

**HOW TO OVERCOME IT**
- Emphasize transferrable skills used in caregiving
- Take some online courses now!
- Convey eagerness to get back to paid work
- Play up since kids are grown, you can focus on career. Then don't mention family again.

Yes, some circumstances can make it more difficult to land a new job, but if you sell yourself confidently with a well-written resume and proactively address the employer's concerns in the interview, you can often make them see what a perfect addition you'd be to their team.

# CHAPTER 10

# Putting Your Plan into Action

N ow that you're prepped and ready to go, it's time to put your job search plan into motion. Consistent effort is key to moving you forward, so try to create a realistic job search schedule that you believe you can stick to. It will be easier to sustain your job search efforts if you balance them with other priorities, so make some time to relax, have fun, exercise and enjoy life.

A set schedule would be best so other things don't creep into your job search time. Take into consideration when you have the most amount of free time and what time of day you tend to be the most productive. If you're not currently employed, I would spend no more than 30 to 40 hours per week on various job search activities. If you are working full-time, you'll have to be creative to find time to dedicate to your job hunt and be highly efficient with your efforts. That's when a step-by-step plan with short specific tasks assigned to each day is the most helpful.

Create a comfortable workspace that's completely dedicated to your job search. It should be a quiet and calming location to which you'll have unrestricted access and that provides privacy with no distractions. Reliable connectivity, a generous number of electrical outlets, space to organize your files and an area suitable for video calls are essential too. Let people know that when you're in your work zone, you're off-limits.

**PRO TIP:** Don't jeopardize your job search by relying on coffee shops, library meeting rooms or communal areas in your home to meet your workspace needs.

Stick to the plan. Consistent effort is the primary factor impacting the success of your job search. You now have a solid, workable plan based on a logical sequence of steps. Complete each step, in order, and you'll see yourself moving closer to your goal. Be sure to celebrate the small victories along the way to help you stay motivated and optimistic. Yes, your ultimate goal is to land a great new job but be proud of yourself for every email sent and phone call made. You'll get there!

To reduce your stress, focus on what you can control — not external factors like non-responses to emails, telephone messages and job applications. Proactive job seekers are focused on what they can impact: the quality of their resume, amount of LinkedIn outreach and networking efforts. There are so many variables in a job search that you need to expect occasional setbacks. But don't let them derail you completely. Recognize that while you're going through a very challenging time, you have what it takes to succeed.

## Job search is tough, but you are tougher!

Lean on your support system. Searching for a job can be one of the most stressful periods in one's life. Having encouraging people around you will help you navigate the emotional roller coaster. Each of us needs a confidential sounding board and trusted advisor at one time or another. Build a reliable network of resources and tell them what you need from them. Most people don't know how to help someone in a job search, so give your friends and family some guidance on what would be most helpful to you.

Many people don't recognize that their well-meaning inquiries and suggestions may be hurtful. The next time someone offers you unsolicited advice, redirect the conversation by simply saying, "Thanks for your input. I'll keep that in mind." Then change the subject. Rather than trying to explain to them the complexity of today's digital job search, just save your energy. When they ask how your job search is going, answer with, "It's going well, thank you." And for the super-rude passive-aggressive, "So, no job yet?" instead of pulling out your hair just respond, "Finding a job is a job in itself. I'm keeping quite busy, thank you." Give a forced smile and move on. It might be helpful to mention to your loved ones that their well-intentioned inquiries put additional pressure on you, and you'd appreciate it if they would respect your wishes and not ask again. Assure them that you'll be glad to share your good news with them when you have it. They may not even realize that they're being insensitive. As long as you deliver this message gently, don't worry too much about their feelings. Your energy would be better spent on self-preservation.

Use the Excel spreadsheet you created earlier to log your efforts and periodically review it to monitor your progress. Looking at the actions you recorded, ask yourself if you've put in consistent, high-quality effort. Have you paid adequate attention to each part of your job search? This monitoring will keep you on track and seeing all that you've accomplished can help sustain your momentum.

Ups and downs are normal; job search success is rarely linear. Periodically evaluate what's been the most effective and where you may have encountered roadblocks. Expect some missteps and prepare to adjust your tactics. If something is working, keep it up; if it's not, find out why and either change it up or stop doing it altogether. What new approach might you take? Have faith in the process and don't second guess every decision you make.

# CHAPTER 11

# Ready, Set, Go!

Well, here we are. I sincerely hope that ***New Rules for the 6-Figure Job Search*** has given you greater confidence and that you now feel prepared for a successful job search and optimistic about your future. You can find more information and the resources I mentioned throughout the book on my website at https://edgecareersolutions.com/book-resources.

I shared these insider secrets to help you gain the competitive edge so you can get noticed, interviewed and hired into a job where you feel good about the work you do. Your career is your story to write, but you can't just show up unprepared and expect to win. Remember, you have to **PLAN** and **PREPARE** before you can **TAKE ACTION.**

If you did complete each step of the process as you read through the book, you are pursuing a job that aligns with who you are personally and professionally; you have an incredibly strong resume, cover letter and LinkedIn profile; you're following a detailed roadmap to get you in front of decision-makers at your target companies and are prepared to ace your job interviews.

However, if you read the book cover to cover to learn about the job search process before proceeding, then it is time to start it again from the beginning and work through the plan. You've got this and I'll be there to guide you every step of the way. Get ready to enjoy a brighter future in a career you love.

I'm in your corner.

*Trish*

# Book Resources

I've created a private page on my website for you, where you'll find *New Rules for the 6-Figure Job Search* resources. Bookmark https://edgecareersolutions.com/book-resources so you can access the tools whenever you need them.

- ⮕ Job Search Checklist
- ⮕ Soft Skills / Hard Skills Exercise
- ⮕ Tasks I Like / What I Never Want To Do Again Exercise
- ⮕ Target Role Exercise
- ⮕ Helpful Websites:
    - » O*NET OnLine (career exploration tools)
    - » CareerOneStop Toolkit (searchable employer database)
    - » Payscale.com (salary research)
    - » Linkup.com (job search engine)
    - » LinkedIn® (professional networking platform)
- ⮕ Compelling Conversation Opener (CCO) Formula
- ⮕ The Challenge-Action-Result (C-A-R) Method for Describing Accomplishments
- ⮕ ATS-Compatibility Resume Formatting Specifics
- ⮕ 500+ of the Best Resume Verbs
- ⮕ Sample Interview Questions
- ⮕ Daily Job Search Planner, Target Company and Tracking Spreadsheets

## About The Author

An executive career coach specializing in senior leadership advancement and mid-career pivots, Trish McGrath has been helping people build more satisfying professional lives since 2009. Equal parts career strategist, content creator and accountability partner, Trish helps C-Suite candidates gain the competitive edge they need to succeed. She understands today's hiring landscape and has grown Edge Career Solutions into a thriving private coaching practice serving a loyal US and Canadian client base across more than 30 industries.

Convinced that there are 'right fit' jobs for each of us, Trish is on a mission to help others succeed in roles they find personally and financially rewarding. Choosing to leave the corporate world for more meaningful work, she learned firsthand that it is never too late to reinvent yourself in a fulfilling encore career. Applying a process-driven approach to executive job search, Trish works 1:1 with each client to solidify their professional brand and position them strategically for their next role. Her direct, no-nonsense approach, collaborative coaching style and exceptional career narratives help her clients get noticed so they get hired into great jobs with their target companies.

Not only does she guide people through their goal setting and job search journeys, Trish also helps them develop tools and skills for lifelong career success. As their strategic partner, Trish provides onboarding support to help rising executives thrive in their new roles and leadership development coaching for ongoing career advancement.

An accomplished resume and profile writer, interview prep coach and LinkedIn trainer, Trish is a recognized subject matter expert in professional branding and overcoming age bias. She shares insider secrets to unlock the hidden job market, teaching her clients how to navigate the new digital job search and build a highly visible online presence to attract the best opportunities.

Over the years, Trish has developed a signature coaching process that empowers her clients to clarify and achieve their career goals. In her book *New Rules for the 6-Figure Job Search*, she encapsulated her successful methods, laying out her professional insights, actionable steps and proven job search strategies in a straightforward step-by-step framework.

Committed to helping others achieve success, Trish volunteers her career coaching services to a variety of non-profit organizations and delivers job search preparedness workshops at local libraries, chambers of commerce, job search groups and universities. She holds a degree in Latin American Studies from the University of Massachusetts-Amherst and is an active member of Career Thought Leaders, The Professional Association of Resume Writers & Career Coaches and Career Directors International. The proud mother of two adult children, Trish resides on Sanibel Island, Florida with her husband and golden retriever.

### You can follow Trish online at:

- https://edgecareersolutions.com
- https://edgecareersolutions.com/blog
- www.linkedin.com/in/trish-thomas-mcgrath
- www.twitter.com/EdgeCareerCoach
- www.facebook.com/EDGECareerSolutions

# Hire Trish as Your
# Personal Career Coach

If a DIY job search is not for you, I am here to help you achieve a successful outcome as your strategic partner. When you retain my coaching services, you will work directly with me, not a subcontractor or less experienced staffer. This personal, 1:1 service differentiates me from my peers and is key to your success.

The career coach / client relationship is one of collaboration built upon trust and mutual respect.

Together, we will position you for success. While I will do the heavy lifting in terms of the writing, I will seek your input as we create your career narrative and branding strategy. When your marketing portfolio is ready, I'll serve as the project manager to focus your job search efforts and keep you moving forward.

I offer a direct approach and a solutions-based coaching model that turns problems into goals. If this sounds like what you need, let's schedule a Discovery Call so we can discuss working together https://calendly.com/career-conversation-with-trish-mcgrath/discovery-call.

---

**As a leader at work, you drive success by filling your team with experts. Why should your approach to managing your career be any different?**

---

# Book Trish to Speak

Trish McGrath has developed a reputation as a 'job search super-hero' for the success she enables her clients to achieve. She enjoys sharing her industry knowledge with others in group presentations, workshops and hands-on LinkedIn training sessions.

What makes Trish stand out as a fan-favorite presenter is her passion for everything career-related. She understands both the employer and job seeker perspectives and knows what it takes to get hired in today's competitive job market.

Over the years, Trish has educated job seekers and business owners in presentations at local libraries, chambers of commerce and trade associations. A mainstay at the Simsbury Public Library and Russell Library in Connecticut for several years, Trish shares valuable insider information that attendees can put to immediate use.

**Educational and Training Workshops** (Live and virtual)

- How to Conduct a Successful Job Search
- Writing a Resume that Will Actually Win Interviews
- Career Pivots: Reinvention, Reentry and Recalibration
- Overcoming Age Bias and Employment Barriers in the Hiring Process
- Interview Success for Leaders
- Accelerating Your Job Search with LinkedIn
- Navigating the Online Job Application Process

- ➲ Identifying Your Ideal Career Path
- ➲ Is Entrepreneurship Right for You?
- ➲ Freelance Consulting: The New "Un-Retirement"
- ➲ How To Grow Your Business with LinkedIn
- ➲ Hands-On LinkedIn Training (in a computer lab)

---

**To learn more about hiring Trish, please visit https://edgecareersolutions.com/workshops.**

---

## About Edge Career Solutions

# EDGE
## CAREER SOLUTIONS

Edge Career Solutions is a private executive career coaching practice serving a wide US and Canadian client base across 30+ industries. Customized coaching programs integrate personal branding campaigns, hard-hitting resume / bio / LinkedIn portfolios and strategic job search plans to accelerate clients' career advancement.

Trish McGrath became a career coach in 2009 because she saw too many people working in jobs that made them miserable. On a mission to help others build happier professional lives, she founded The Resume Resource to fill the void between high-end consulting firms and the generic resume mills that don't actually help job seekers. Trish delivered exceptional results for her clients and quickly became a reputable resource for job seekers at all levels of experience.

Over the years, as job seekers' needs changed with the new digital job market, Trish completed more advance training and expanded her service offerings to include career planning, personal branding, interview prep, coaching for rising leaders and LinkedIn optimization. In 2015, Trish rebranded her company as EDGE Career Solutions to represent her end-to-end career management services and later moved the CT-based practice to Sanibel Island, FL. As a Certified Career Transition coach, MBTI® practitioner and hidden job market expert, Trish helps people build professional careers that are personally and financially rewarding.

---

**To learn more about Edge Career Solutions coaching programs and how Trish can help you gain the competitive edge you need to succeed, please visit https://edgecareersolutions.com.**

---

www.ingramcontent.com/pod-product-compliance
Lightning Source LLC
Chambersburg PA
CBHW071703210326
41597CB00017B/2310